on track ...

Thin Lizzy

every album, every song

Graeme Stroud

SONICBOND

sonicbondpublishing.com

Sonicbond Publishing Limited
www.sonicbondpublishing.co.uk
Email: info@sonicbondpublishing.co.uk

First Published in the United Kingdom 2020
First Published in the United States 2020

British Library Cataloguing in Publication Data:
A Catalogue record for this book is available from the British Library

Copyright Graeme Stroud 2020

ISBN 978-1-78952-064-4

Typeset in ITC Garamond & ITC Avant Garde
Printed and bound in England

Graphic design and typesetting: Full Moon Media

on track ...
Thin Lizzy

every album, every song

Graeme Stroud

sonicbondpublishing.com

Acknowledgements

The author would like to offer profuse thanks to everyone who helped in compiling this information, including the fanatical fans who support the forums and maintain so many musical websites, blogs, and online commentaries.

The following people merit particular attention:
Stephen Lambe, Brian Stroud, Jim Fitzpatrick, Dirk Sommer and Larry Canavan and everybody at VelvetThunder.co.uk, especially Lee Vickers and Steve Pilkington. And, of course, my wife Caro and our children, Lorelei and Haslem, for getting right behind the project and giving it their unflagging support – thanks and love.

A special shout to John Crookes for going above and beyond! Thanks, John!

Extra special thanks to Brian Downey.

Honourable mentions and heartfelt thanks to all of the following:
Adriano Di Ruscio, Alain Pacaud, Andy Fox, Anthony Booth, Chris Puttock, Colin Hunt, Des Moloney, Glen Prince, Jack van Dijk, Marcel Hartenberg, Jim Cameron, John Carreiro, Justin Young, Keith Campbell, Kevin Curran, Malc Leese, Mats Andersson, Mick Morton, Mike Mooney, Neil Ford, Rade Hendrix, Scott Glazier, Scotty Johnson, Stacy Williamson, Steen Bugtrup, Stephen Gardner, Steve Morris and Trevor Raggatt.

on track ...

Thin Lizzy

Contents

Introduction

With its back against the wall of the Atlantic Ocean and its face towards Britain and the vast sweep of the Eurasian continent beyond, Ireland is an outsider, the last outpost of Western Europe. Steeped in the musical tradition of Gaelic folk, Ireland has nevertheless contributed some stellar characters to the history of rock, in which the name of Thin Lizzy looms large. And when discussing the rock band Thin Lizzy, it is no mistake to concentrate heavily on its instigator, lyricist and public-facing persona, the late Philip Lynott.

Someone in the market for a Thin Lizzy record or CD will usually be directed to the section marked 'Hard Rock/Metal', or something similar. Thin Lizzy were a rock band, but their forays into real hard rock territory were few and far between, mostly in their latter days. Their back catalogue covered everything from melodic rock to soul, prog, folk, fusion and romantic balladry – to concentrate on their hard rock endeavours is to miss out most of their enviable history. Phil Lynott, a fatherless half-caste in a strictly Catholic country, lived bright and fast like a shooting star and burned himself prematurely into oblivion in an atmosphere of alcohol and hard drugs. His early work, though, reveals the soul of a poet.

The circumstances that brought the Lynotts or their ancestors to the Emerald Isle at some point in misty history, creating their character and personality, belong in another book. Still, we must pick up the story at some point, and strange as it may seem when opening the book on this most Irish of bands, we begin not in the Lynott family's home city of Dublin, nor in the green and grassy Republic of Ireland at all, but in the English industrial heartland city of Birmingham. Thence a teenaged Dublin girl named Philomena Lynott had fled to find work in the aftermath of the most devastating war in history, and there she met and dallied briefly with a man named Cecil Parris from British Guiana. For a young, inexperienced and virginal Catholic girl to break as many taboos as she did is astonishing, nevertheless, she became intimate enough with the older, black foreigner for their brief relationship to leave Philomena pregnant. For sure, the trauma of the Second World War had blunted or demolished many taboos and perhaps excused a radical change in behaviour among the survivors, but tradition was still a mighty foe and Philomena, alone in a foreign country, kept the pregnancy secret from her distant family right up until the birth.

Her son Philip Parris Lynott was born on 20th August 1949 on English soil, at a hospital in West Bromwich near Birmingham. Philomena chased work and accommodation around the Midlands of England, infant in tow, but Philip at four years of age was at last sent back to Crumlin, a district of Dublin, to live with his grandparents Frank and Sarah Lynott.

It is difficult to imagine how this would seem in the staunchly Catholic capital of the Republic of Ireland in the days after the war. An illegitimate, motherless black child could conceivably be the target of all kinds of Dickensian oppression, but incredibly, it seems that although Philomena had suffered degradation and oppression in England for her lifestyle – in fact, she had two more children out of wedlock, both of whom were given up for adoption – Philip was accepted by his family, by his peers and by the community at large in Ireland. He was foreign-looking for sure, exotic even, and the differences were not lost on him, but he escaped any severe persecution and in fact grew up to be cool and popular, black and Irish, "like a pint of Guinness," as he famously quipped.

Phil got into music at an early age, bought a guitar and also discovered that a boy in a lower year at his school, one Brian Downey, played the drums. While still in their mid-teens, the two lads started playing together up and down the country in a covers band by the name of The Black Eagles, who were good enough to have a Manager and everything. After that combo petered out, Phil went more avant-garde with a band named Kama Sutra, but then success looked in his direction when he was invited by bassist Brendan 'Brush' Shiels to front his new band Skid Row. Lynott wasn't quite 18 when Skid Row played their first gig, but from the point of view of later Lizzy fans, things got even more interesting when guitarist Bernard Cheevers quit the band for a full-time job in civvy street. His replacement was a 16-year-old guitar wizard from the other side of the border in Belfast, named Gary Moore.

Skid Row recorded one single with Lynott singing, a folky, dreamy acoustic guitar ballad named 'New Faces, Old Places', with a swinging jazz number named 'Misdemeanour Dream Felicity' on the B-side. As fate would have it, Lynott had to take a break to have his tonsils removed; during the hiatus, Shiels took over the frontman duties and Lynott was effectively given the push, leaving Skid row as a trio with Moore on guitar and Noel Bridgeman on drums. Shiels softened the pill though, giving Lynott one of his bass guitars and teaching him how to play.

Armed with his rudimentary new instrumental skills, Lynott was invited to join Brian Downey's blues band Sugar Shack, who had recorded one successful single in Ireland, a cover of Tim Rose's 'Morning Dew' (originally written and recorded by Bonnie Dobson), with a cover of Cream's 'Sunshine Of Your Love' on the B-side. Coincidentally, Sugar Shack were once supported by a band named Platform Three, which featured a very youthful Gary Moore on guitar.

When the Sugar Shack project splintered, Lynott and Downey formed a new band named Orphanage, with Joe Staunton on guitar and Pat Quigley on bass, until Lynott later took over bass himself. And this, as they say, is where the story really starts. Orphanage were, by all accounts, an ill-disciplined and loose amalgamation of several musicians, any of whom may or may not turn up on any given night. However, popular legend has it that they impressed another Belfast guitarist one night during a pub gig in Dublin.

Eric Bell was only a couple of years older than Lynott, but among a stack of other bands, he had played in an outfit named Shades of Blue and was briefly a member of Them, fronted by singer Van Morrison. Bell was prowling Dublin with keyboard player Eric Wrixon, another former member of Them, looking for decent musicians to form a new band, and when they found a local gig, they went along – the band on stage was Orphanage. Massively impressed both by Lynott's lyricism and on-stage presence, and Downey's superb drumming, Bell went backstage after the gig and asked the two lads right there and then whether they would be interested in starting a band with him and Wrixon. They had heard of Bell, who had trodden the same circuit as Gary Moore in Belfast, and agreed. The new four-piece eventually settled on the name Thin Lizzy after a 1950s character named Tin Lizzie from the *Dandy* comic.

The name itself is worth some attention. The original Tin Lizzie was an unofficial name for the classic Model T Ford motor car, the first car to be built using mass-production techniques in the early 1900s. In 1922, a driver named Noel Bullock entered a battered Model T which he had nicknamed 'Old Liz' into a race in Colorado, USA. The beaten-up old relic was assigned the nickname 'Tin Lizzie', and actually won the race, which cemented the reputation of the cheap Model T as a durable, reliable workhorse of a motor, and the name Tin Lizzie became well-publicised in the national press.

The *Dandy* created a story in 1953 about a robot housemaid named Tin Lizzie after the old car. She originally appeared as a prose character but was soon promoted to a picture strip, drawn by an artist named Jack Prout. In conversation with the author, Brian Downey explained how the name came to be applied to their new band:

> One day we were sitting in the Countdown Club in Dublin when we were starting off, and I think it was Eric Bell who came up with the idea of Tin Lizzie, like the comic spelling. It was on a kind of a shortlist, and I remember sitting there going 'Nah, that doesn't sound too good…' We went through another few names, but for some reason, we kept coming back. The next day we came back to it as well, because we were trying for a few days to find a name. Then Eric came up with the idea of putting the 'h' in. He said, 'Well in Dublin, nobody pronounces the 'th' anyway, so it would just be a little bit of a joke.' I think we did a couple of gigs calling ourselves Thin Lizzie with an 'ie'. But we put the word out to promoters that we had changed the name again, it's not 'ie' it's 'y', but promoters still used the 'ie' for ages it seemed. But it was Eric Bell who came up with the idea; like myself, he was a Beano aficionado. We used to have comics in the van going to gigs as well; we were big comic guys.

The spelling was changed from Lizzie to Lizzy before they hit the big time, but they were still Lizzie when their first single was released.

In any case, both Orphanage and Bell were well-known enough for the new band, almost a supergroup in today's terms, to be hotly anticipated, and their formation was announced in the press. Recollections differ as to where their first gig was played; either a school hall in Cloghran or in St Anthony's Hall in Clontarf. Downey clearly recollects it as the Cloghran venue, but is aware that there is some disagreement, as he explains:

I think it was Cloghran, it was outside of Dublin as far as I remember. A lot of people do remember that gig in St. Anthony's Hall though, including our ex-Manager Terry O'Neill, who mentioned to me years ago that was our first gig, though I always had the idea that we played in Cloghran first. I think maybe we could have done a quick half-hour in St. Anthony's, a really quick gig, because I really can't remember it, and then maybe played the official gig at Cloghran? So I'm not really sure, but it's definitely one of those two gigs!

The four-piece dossed together in the upper floor of a block in Clontarf, on the seaward side of Dublin, close to the castle that would feature on their first album. They managed to wangle some free time at the new Trend studio by promising to record a song written by the owner, John D'Ardis. The song was called 'I Need You' and ended up as the B-side to their debut single, a Lynott composition named 'The Farmer', released under the name Thin Lizzie in 1970. Parlophone had been talking about signing the band, but the single flopped as debut singles shall, selling less than 300 copies, and the label bailed. Eric Wrixon left the band before the single was released and floated around Europe before eventually rejoining his previous band Them. Thin Lizzy were now evolving into a guitar-based power trio on the template of Cream, Ten Years After, or The Jimi Hendrix Experience.

Lizzy was being managed at this time by Terry O'Neill, who was finding it difficult to stump up the necessary cash to keep the band buoyant. He approached a local music shop owner named Brian Tuite about co-managing the band, but in the event, Tuite teamed up with Peter Bardon, who provided the financial clout, to take on the job. Tuite was friends with one of Decca's A&R men, and arranged for him to come and view a soul singer named Ditch Cassidy – but replaced Cassidy's usual backing band with Thin Lizzy. Decca signed Cassidy to one of their subsidiaries to do a single, but Lizzy ended up with a full recording contract. Thanks to Tuite, it was the start of the big adventure, as they relocated to London to record their debut album.

Thin Lizzy

Released: UK 30 April 1971, US 14 July 1971
Label: Decca (London in US)
Recorded at: Decca Studios, West Hampstead, London, January 1971
Philip Lynott: Vocals, bass guitar, rhythm guitar, acoustic guitar
Eric Bell: Lead guitar, twelve-string guitar
Brian Downey: Drums, percussion
Ivor Raymonde: Mellotron on 'Honesty Is No Excuse'
Produced by: Scott English
Album duration: 39 minutes
This album did not chart

Recorded over the course of five days at Decca's West Hampstead studio, in a smoky haze of dope as was *de rigeur* at the time, Thin Lizzy's debut long-player was released on 30 April 1971, with the band name corrected to the current spelling. Radio 1's ever-reliable mentor of new talent John Peel contributed some airplay, and Radio Luxembourg's Kid Jensen got right behind it immediately, but there are few if any hummable melody lines or hooks, and nothing really for the commercial record-buying public to get hold of. The free-form nature of the singing seems to have freed the musician side of the band from any constraints though – they, therefore, weave complex, trippy and ambient strands of anything that comes to mind, and the lyrics are laid gently on top like a sleeping princess.

There was obviously no point in hammering away at the tunes with straight 4/4 rock precision, so Downey plays the drums like a musical instrument; his imaginative percussion manages to make the drums a part of the instrumentation rather than a solid base from which to launch an aural attack. It's quite challenging to pigeonhole the musical style; in fact, it is more prog-folk than rock.

Truthfully though, based on this first offering, it's difficult to see how the early band had garnered such an awesome reputation for their hard-rocking live shows. This set is quiet and introspective, even cerebral, and shows Lynott not as a rocker, not even as a songwriter *per se,* but purely and simply as a poet. True, that was the way of contemporary Irish music in the '60s and early '70s, and it is easy to imagine some of these songs being crooned by Van Morrison, but less easy to imagine them in the hands of any of the power trios mentioned earlier. Lynott loves to spotlight specific characters by name in his songs, and plenty of locals get a mention on this set.

Album cover

Decca's art department delved into their archive and pulled out an ingenious photo-collage to use on the cover, credited to David Wedgbury. A photo is taken with a fisheye lens at extremely close quarters of the headlight of a rather dilapidated 1950s motor car in an urban street. The car's headlight has had another wide-angle photo carefully superimposed on top of it, of apparently the same car from a different angle. The whole melange is placed in a circular frame that takes up most of the cover, with a black background and the words 'Thin Lizzy' picked out in bright yellow in the top-left. The band were asked to approve it, while at the same time being told that there was no alternative. "Whether we had given permission or not, I think they would have still used it," said Brian Downey. "It's not a brilliant photograph for the first album by any means, but we had no say in the matter, we had to go along with it." Whatever the technical or artistic merits of the shot, its grimy urban vibe didn't really make it a must-buy. It is tempting to assume the location is a Dublin backstreet, but in fact, a distant road name-board indicates that the photo was taken in England because the street sign has a white background – Irish road names have a green background. The car (for those who wish to know), is a 1957/58 Vauxhall Victor 'F' Series. A completely different sleeve design was used for the US release – a primitive cartoon car is shown careering over a hill which is actually a woman's naked thigh. Go figure, as they say Stateside.

'The Friendly Ranger At Clontarf Castle' (Bell, Lynott 3:02)

It's clear from the opener that Thin Lizzy had no aspirations for the first bars of their first album to hit anybody like a sledgehammer. The title itself is clearly intended to convey gentle, good-humoured relaxation rather than anything approaching rock. Downey leads off with a gentle tom rhythm that pans deeply from left to right with Bell strumming some ambient chords; Lynott recites a short poem about the ranger in prose as a kind of intro. After a minute or so, the song proper comes in, with Phil singing more, thematically-related poetry over some sweet, deeply-phased chords and staccato bass. Over the course of a mere three minutes, the band drops in and out at will, with Bell playing an overdubbed four-part guitar melody line over a sparse backing at one point – eat your heart out Brian May! The boys spent some time living in a crash pad in the Clontarf district of Dublin which they dubbed Clontarf Castle, down the road as it was from the actual castle itself, but the friendly ranger was Lynott's pet cat Pippin, whose face markings put Phil in mind of the Lone Ranger. Lynott would go on to name his music publishing company *Pippin The Friendly Ranger*.

'Honesty Is No Excuse' (Lynott 3:40)

The first track stops and this one comes straight in without a break. Musically along similar lines, nevertheless, there is a stylistic change as Lynott sings a complex lyric line in a notably high key. It's pure Van Morrison at this point. Acoustic guitar strumming and heavy use of the string section underpin a complex and musical number, with Mellotron contributed by session musician Ivor Raymonde, better known as a jazz, classical and big band pianist, before he went on to become a music director at the BBC. There is an interesting conflict, or comparison perhaps, between the lyrics and the title: the singer lays bare his soul, confessing to using one who loved him for his own pleasure and comfort, while singing 'Honesty was my only excuse' at the end of every verse. In the title, he simply states that it wasn't a good enough reason, 'Honesty Is No Excuse'. Judge as you see fit. Raymonde, we are told, loved the song.

'Diddy Levine' (Lynott 7:06)

More acoustic strumming introduces this ballad, while Lynott sings a narrative poem in a semi-speaking style. It's a kind of reality show sung to music, following the lives of Eunice King (who is a bloke), and his common-law wife Diddy Levine, who has a daughter named Janice from a previous marriage. A complex tale follows Janice as she grows up, and specifically mentions everyone by name. The song takes up three minutes, then unexpectedly morphs into a two-minute free-form Cream-type jam, with a guitar in the right channel playing the riff, while another in the left channel plays solo. The last two minutes extract a moral from the tale along the lines of the-more-things-change-the-more-they-stay-the-same, pushing the whole piece to seven minutes.

'Ray-Gun' (Bell 3:06)

Ah, now, here is a proper rock song, starting with a groovy Robin Trower type riff with deep wah, then the band comes in with a funky backing and heavily reverb-soaked lead guitar in the left channel. Quite clearly, if Lynott was the poet with his head in the clouds, Bell was the rocker. The science-fiction aspect is a bit of a red herring here; although the song speaks of someone from another planet, who carries a ray gun, the planet is specifically said to be only 3,000 miles away, and one gets the distinct impression we are talking about an American, probably carrying a run-of-the-mill handgun. The foreigner is castigated right from the start for having no religion, kicking off a theme that would recur time and again over the lifetime of the band. Multiple guitar lines tend to overwhelm the vocals, to be honest, but it's a welcome breath of life in a pretty pedestrian set. It is also one of the very few Lizzy-penned songs not to have Lynott's name on the writing credits at all.

'Look What The Wind Blew In' (Lynott 3:23)

This is a jazz-chorded but staccato rock-rhythmed up-tempo piece with guitars tending to overwhelm the vocals again. The contemplative lyrics tell of a man who has had lots of lovers without fear or conscience, but now finds himself afraid due to a 'gale from the north'. The gale that flew in, (not blew in as in the title), was Lynott's current paramour, one Gale Barber from Belfast in Northern Ireland, who had moved from Ireland to London with Phil and lived with him in West Hampstead. It is certainly an energetic song, with an unaccompanied vocal chorus hook born for audience interaction.

15

'Eire' (Lynott 2:07)

Lynott sings a poem concerning Celts versus Vikings set to a gorgeously ambient but surprisingly complex backing of acoustic and reverb-soaked electric guitars, tom rolls and melodic bass runs. A decently rocking guitar solo fades out barely 2 minutes into the song, which is a shame. The storyline is a bit confusing as it is in two halves separated by hundreds of years. First, it speaks lyrically of the land of Eireann, one of the many variants for the country's name now usually spelt Eire, and the High King's fight against the 'dreaded Vikings' – probably High King Brian Boru's defence against the picturesquely-named Sigtrygg Silkbeard and his Norse allies of Orkney and the Isle of Man at the battle of Clontarf in 1014. 'Of course,' I hear you cry. But then it name-checks Red O'Donnell and Hugh O'Neill, two heroes in the wars against the English, 'the Saxon foe' of Tudor times. The purpose is to cast Eire in a heroic role, as a sturdy opponent of oppression – Lynott was keen to sing the lyrics in Irish Gaelic, and reportedly recorded a take in that language, but that was a step too far for Decca and he re-did it in English.

'Return Of The Farmer's Son' (Downey, Lynott 4:13)

The power trio makes an appearance here; a hard-rocking intro in Cream style with a descending guitar riff and deep bass – this is probably the first introduction to the later Lizzy style, portending songs such as 'Emerald' still to come. More poetic content tells of a wayward son proclaiming his love for his widowed father, a good-hearted, hard-working farmer. The singer reminisces about his strictly religious father who would 'smack him on the ass' to get him to church.

'Clifton Grange Hotel' (Lynott 2:27)

A rim-shot, restrained, almost dance-band drum pattern underscores heavily overdriven guitar. The hotel of the title is not actually mentioned by name in the song, but was a real premises in Manchester run by Philomena Lynott and her partner Dennis Keeley throughout the late '60s and '70s. Known locally as 'The Showbiz' or just 'The Biz', the hotel's clientele were mostly showbiz folk or local celebrities, notably Manchester United footballers. Lynott got to know George Best here, a legend of Manchester United and Northern Ireland and certainly one of the most famous footballers of his generation. The short track name-checks a few regular customers, but basically fades out when they run out of stuff to do.

'Saga Of The Ageing Orphan' (Lynott 3:40)

This song has another gorgeous, ambient intro with two acoustic guitars playing harmonising arpeggios. Minimal jazz-brush drums and restrained bass underlie a poem about an ordinary family; Lynott's uncle Peter is named specifically, reading a book while his mother, Lynott's grandmother, cooks. In Lynott's way, the song merges autobiographical details with a misty-eyed

16

nostalgia, seasoned with a twist of sadness. It's a short poem about the inevitability of ageing, but really it's all about the music, with some flamenco-influenced guitar in parts. The number does not escalate at all, but is beautiful throughout, with a rising bass line to finish.

'Remembering' (Lynott 6:00)
There is a trip once around the toms to start, and the listener can just hear the final syllable of something spoken, as if someone was talking over the intro and they forgot to edit it out. The intro seems to be unrelated to the actual number, which alternates between quiet passages of nostalgic reminiscence and louder passages of bitter realisation. In the quiet passages, the singer reminisces with misty nostalgia about his first girlfriend, when the pair were just children. In the louder sections, he ruefully points out how the two of them have changed so much, and how the old days are lost but not forgotten. Then, at about four minutes, a free-form bass section leads into a psychedelic hard rock dual guitar wig-out with two guitar solos playing at once, one just overdriven, one with overdrive and wah, which gets harder and harder towards the end, eventually finishing on a tight drum and bass crash. This is getting remarkably close to fusion rock. On later editions of the vinyl and on most CD issues, the *New Day* EP is tacked on to the end of the record, with its song 'Remembering (Part Two)', and this song is rebranded as 'Remembering (Part One)'.

Associated material
'The Farmer' (Lynott 3:37)
An Ireland-only release on the Parlophone label on 30 July 1970 before the band signed with Decca, this was Thin Lizzy's first single, recorded at Trend Studio in Baggott Street, Dublin, under the name Thin Lizzie. This drawling western country ballad is underpinned by Eric Wrixon's Hammond and piano and sets a scene that Lynott would come back to again and again: a cowboy song, a tale of outlaws of the old west. Lynott starts with a spoken section where he puns on the band's name, saying "I do appreciate y'all comin' – specially you Skinny Lizzy!" No farmer is ever mentioned in this song, which concerns a wake held for the protagonist's mother, including whiskey bought with the proceeds of a bank heist. This song was eventually included on the 2010 expanded CD version of the debut album.

'I Need You' (D'Ardis 4:06)
Released on 30 July 1970 as the B-side of the above single, this song features a decent but relatively standard, disappointed love-lyric written by the studio owner John D'Ardis (spelt 'Dardis' on the record). A horn section introduces an up-tempo rock'n'roller with tinkling piano. Some groovy drum rolls and great guitar soloing contribute to what is actually a really good, and surprisingly lengthy 1960s pop song, which would have been a hit if Georgie Fame or Alan Price had done it. It doesn't sound much like Thin Lizzy because

17

it simply isn't – D'Ardis and some mates had already recorded the backing track and it was presented as a fait accompli; Lynott added the vocals written by D'Ardis and Bell overdubbed some guitar parts.

'New Day' EP

Released 20 August 1971. The fact is that *Thin Lizzy* the album didn't sell in anything like the numbers Decca demanded of their burgeoning stars, and they weren't of a mind to bankroll a second effort without wringing the cloth out a bit more. They ended up agreeing to a four-track EP, which was recorded at Decca's West Hampstead studios in June 1971 and was released as *New Day* on 20 August – it didn't really do any better than the album, but it didn't do any worse either, and the standard was good enough to convince Decca to agree to a second full-length offering. CD editions of the first album tend to include the four EP songs as bonus tracks, so they have become associated in many people's minds with that record, but in some ways, they have more in common with the next LP, especially as production duties were handled by Nick Tauber, as on the next two albums. Tauber had actually been involved in mixing the first album in an uncredited capacity, but perhaps the most momentous thing about *New Day* was that it represents the first professional album cover art from one Rodney Matthews, who would go on to create classic artwork for a whole raft of stars from the New Wave Of British Heavy Metal, and Magnum in particular. Lizzy had played a college gig in Bristol and a local booking agent mentioned Matthews' name. At the college, a poster he had done for another gig took their eye, but Decca refused to shell out for a picture sleeve, so Lizzy financed it themselves – a jolly-faced sun peers above the horizon in a cartoonish fashion reminiscent of The Beatles' *Yellow Submarine* art, a style pretty well unrecognisable from Matthews' later work. The songs from the EP are listed below…

'Dublin' (Lynott 2:26)

From the *New Day* EP, another wistful poem about lost love, tied in with a wistful nostalgia over the city itself that Lynott left behind. No bass or drums feature on this track, just intimate vocals over acoustic guitar, with a heavily-reverbed electric guitar in the background – in fact, Lynott recorded it on one occasion with no musical backing at all, simply as spoken poetry. Rod Mayall contributes some celeste to this musical version, which sounds a bit like a glockenspiel in the intro.

'Remembering (Part Two): New Day' (Downey, Bell 5:05)

From the *New Day* EP, up-tempo folk-rock with rapid backing, nothing to do with the original 'Remembering', except in so far as it turns over a new leaf and contemplates the future with optimism. The band messes about with the timing somewhat; it misses a beat at the end of each section, playing a shorter bar. There is no conventional drum kit on this one, but wicked high tom or timbale work all the way through, and some pretty nifty guitar shredding. This could be a potentially great live track, but the vocals are mixed low for some reason. It is easy to hear the origins of some later folk-rock acts; The Waterboys come to mind.

'Old Moon Madness' (Lynott 3:53)

From the *New Day* EP, an up-tempo psychedelic backing in 3/4 time backs a spoken-word poem regarding a werewolf, with occasional howling effects thrown in. There is some lovely, neat proggy bass-and-guitar fast riffage and a nice solo on this one, following the chords, which don't naturally follow each other in a standard key. This is full-on prog really, with stunning musicianship, but the poem is definitely structured as prose, without relation to the backing. We are treated to a big bass section towards the end, with up-tempo dual guitar backing, then a sudden tight ending halfway through the fadeout! This should have made it on to the album really. Lynott draws the moral that, never mind what gruesome crimes you may have committed as a werewolf during the night; plenty of worse things have been done 'with no moon madness to blame it on.'

'Things Ain't Working Out Down At The Farm' (Lynott 4:29)

From the *New Day* EP, a swinging, light-hearted look at the hypocrisy of a Bible-carrying drunk, amongst other characters. The song builds to a full-on screamer with monotone rhythm guitar and wah soloing, with a drum solo passage and bluesy crash ending. The most notable sections are when the music stops completely and Lynott sings solo with his heavily-accented drawl, 'Things ain't working ouwiiiit – down at the farm.'

'Mama And Papa' (Lynott 2:25)

This unreleased song was recorded in 1970 at the Trend Studios sessions, but didn't make the album cut and eventually surfaced on an EP named *Philip Lynott – The Lost Recordings* that was given away as a promo with Dublin-based magazine *Hot Press* in August 2010. The EP featured five songs from the sessions, three of which appeared (as different versions) either on the first album or the *New Day* EP, but with two previously-unreleased songs, including this one and the song below...

'It's Really Worthwhile' (Lynott 3:22)

With the above, these were the two previously-unreleased songs to appear on the EP named *Philip Lynott – The Lost Recordings* that was given away as a promo with Dublin-based magazine Hot Press in August 2010.

Shades Of A Blue Orphanage

Released: UK 10 March 1972, (not released in US)
Label: Decca
Recorded at: De Lane Lea Music Centre, Wembley, London, 1971
Philip Lynott: Vocals, bass guitar, rhythm guitar, acoustic guitar
Eric Bell: Lead guitar, acoustic guitar
Brian Downey: Drums, percussion
Clodagh Simonds: Harpsichord, keyboards, mellotron
Produced by: Nick Tauber
Album duration: 40 minutes
This album did not chart

The EP was good enough to convince Decca to bankroll a new album, which
was recorded at De Lane Lea studios in Wembley. Pretty similar to the first
album in terms of content, it features more of Lynott's poetry over fairly
freeform backings, but reportedly no one in the band was really happy with
it. And there we have the curse of the 'difficult second album' – clearly, any
band that has been gigging for a while is going to select the best of its existing
repertoire for their debut, which means that the second-rate stuff is mostly
going to find its way on to the second, plus hopefully enough decent new
material to keep the average up. Eric Bell reported that: 'A lot of the second
album was made up in the studio, there and then.'

Probably the most interesting thing about the album is the name –
Orphanage, of course, was the name of Lynott and Downey's previous band,
and it has already been mentioned that Bell had played in a band named
Shades Of Blue. Combined with Phil's poetic song about 'The Ageing Orphan'
on the first album, this title is a clever piece of work. Whether the song or the
album title came first is not known, but the album closes with the title track,
a nostalgic ballad about teenage pastimes, dreaming the time away at the
pictures or the snooker hall.

Ted Carroll had been drafted in by Tuite and Bardon as another co-manager,
and he also managed Northern Irish keyboard player Clodagh Simonds from
the band Mellow Candle. Clodagh contributed some keyboard backings to the
album and went on to guest on several Mike Oldfield albums.

Album cover

The sleeve design continues the gritty, urban theme of their debut, utilising
a library photograph of three street urchins, two of them barefoot, standing
on the pavement in front of a plain brick wall. The fact that there are three
of them is the photo's only relationship to the band. The back cover shows
a monochrome photo of the band strolling through St. Stephen's Green in
Dublin on a rainy day, Downey holding an umbrella. However, the company
did lash out for a gatefold, which seems remarkably extravagant of them – the
inner spread contains all the album credits, and also exhibits another black and

white photo of the boys on the same wet and wild day, standing up to their ankles in water. Welcome to Ireland, people.

'The Rise And Dear Demise Of the Funky Nomadic Tribes'
(Lynott, Bell, Downey 7:06)
This track starts with a pretty groovy 45-second drum pattern, which culminates in a section straight from 'Jailbreak'. This then launches into a funky soul number, very complex, but not over-tight by today's standards. Lynott's voice is gruff and soulful. There is an extended, heavy drum, fadeout section reminiscent of 'Sha-La-La' still to come, which is really good but not what you would expect for an opening track. The words are pretty surreal, telling a loose story of how the nomadic tribes in question were destroyed by encroachment from 'a European'.

'Buffalo Gal' (Lynott 5:30)
A Van Morrison-ish folk pop song with acoustic guitar, some keyboards and some unusual time signature changes. The 'buffalo girl' motif implies that this is a western-based idea, but there's actually nothing in the lyric to suggest that except the word 'buffalo' and the statement that the gal in question knew Jesse James' middle name, which was Woodson by the way.

'I Don't Want To Forget How To Jive' (Lynott 1:46)
A really weird one this, with Lynott doing a kind of rudimentary Elvis impersonation over some really clunky minor-key honky-tonk piano and choppy clear-toned guitar. The words are mostly indecipherable and what is audible is mostly nonsensical. Then it fades out after a minute and a half, which is a mercy, frankly.

'Sarah' (Lynott 2:59)
This glorious ode, in stark contrast to the previous number, starts with bird song, then some ethereal piano from Clodagh Simonds that fades in through the reverb over some really ambient acoustic arpeggios. You would never expect this from Lynott or Lizzy, it's actually beautiful, with double-tracked vocals. It's naturally assumed to be about Lynott's maternal grandmother Sarah who raised him during a fair part of his childhood, but the lyric is fairly opaque and again the words are lost in the production. Even if the lyric does not directly and literally apply to his grandmother, the choice of name is by no means coincidental, and the singer's deep affection overflows in the poetry. The most unusual thing about the song is that Thin Lizzy would record another Lynott composition with the same title a few albums later; an ode to his first daughter, named Sarah in honour of her great-grandmother.

'Brought Down' (Lynott 4:19)
More hippy folk stuff with two acoustic guitars. The lyrics are very specific about the year: 'I was seldom sober in nineteen-hundred-and-fifty-four.' Lynott

would have been 4 or 5 years old in that year, so it's not autobiographical – the only connection I can track down would relate to Lynott's Catholic roots, as 1954 was a 'Marian Year', as declared by Pope Pius XII. A Marian Year is specifically dedicated to the Virgin Mary and can theoretically be declared at any time, but in actual fact 1954 was the first time it had ever been done, making it a momentous year in Ireland. This song also includes the line 'my baby had a baby by me,' so draw whatever conclusions you like about the virgin birth and immaculate conception – or more prosaically it could have been a reference to his own father. It was even more personal than that though, as Lynott had himself fathered a secret son, given up for adoption, in 1969 with then-girlfriend Carole Stephen. The 'My baby had a baby' line is interesting inasmuch as it appears on the later *Live and Dangerous* album, interpolated into the song 'Still In Love With You', the only representation from this album. There is a bit of experimentation with track volumes in this one, as really loud backing vocals bring in the band, who also experiment with some proggy time signatures. Lynott added overdubs to this sparse version to create a much fuller sound on the version released in 1977 on the spruced-up compilation album *The Continuing Saga Of The Ageing Orphans.* Incidentally, some may be wondering why a specifically pious, religious observance would cause someone to be rarely sober for a whole year. In Ireland, most celebrations are tied in with the church calendar in some way or other, and any excuse for a drink-up is allegedly considered acceptable.

'Baby Face' (Lynott 3:27)
A psychedelic riff-driven hard rocker with an erotic edge; Lynott growling with intensity and Bell drawing the feedback out of multiple guitars in the background. There are some really neat, proggy timing artefacts towards the fadeout.

'Chatting Today' (Lynott 4:19)
Acoustic guitars with maracas or some such percussion play an up-tempo 3/4 Latin rhythm, but the backing has nothing to do with the lyrics and there is no tune at all. It's a half-sung but mostly spoken poem about leaving the edges of church life, going on to various jobs, but always ending up living and sleeping on the railway. No bass again on this one, but Bell noodles away quietly on acoustic lead lines. This was actually an older number that wasn't recorded for the first album but was drafted in to help flesh out the second.

'Call The Police' (Lynott 3:37)
This number features a loud, raucous rock backing, but the vocals are fairly restrained and bordering on rap. A basic lyric about a shady character recalls 'Bad Reputation', but here we have the first mention of a character named Johnny who would appear (in name at least) on several later songs, and also someone called Thin Miss Lizzy. It finishes on a police siren – one of the wailing American ones, not a 1970s British ne-na.

'Shades Of a Blue Orphanage' (Lynott 7:06)

Reverb-soaked ambient chords with a gentle drum rhythm lie underneath a dreamy-eyed, nostalgic poem about teenage life. Again, there is no tune as such, and the words are about as obscure as they can get, evoking scenes from Lynott's childhood in a misty-eyed nostalgic haze. The poetic musing drifts into waltz-time extended atmosphere at the end with some old country harmonica buzzing in the background. It also sounds like there are some female vocals in the choruses, but they are not credited.

Associated material
Funky Junction Play a Tribute to Deep Purple

Incredibly, Thin Lizzy was hired by a producer and entrepreneur named Dave Miller (aka Leo Muller) to record a cover album of Deep Purple songs. As Purple's sound featured the high piercing screams of vocalist Ian Gillan and was notably heavy on the distorted Hammond organ of Jon Lord, the Thin Lizzy trio would not seem to have been an obvious fit for the task – especially seeing as another Dublin band named Elmer Fudd regularly covered Deep Purple songs to a high standard in their set. Fudd's frontman Benny White and their keyboard player Dave Lennox were duly brought in to complete the sound and the new band dubbed Funky Junction. The entire set was rehearsed and recorded in one day, which is no mean feat, but also necessarily included some non-Purple padding. The band members were not credited anywhere on the album and the blurry stage shot on the cover is of a different band completely; often stated to be Hard Stuff who were signed to the Deep Purple label Purple Records. For those who wish to know, the resulting record was named *Funky Junction Play a Tribute to Deep Purple* and was released on the UK Stereo Gold Award label on 2 March 1973. The name of the band was changed to The Rock Machine for the German market, and just to add to the confusion, Miller knocked together a completely different group, also named Funky Junction, to play on another of his projects later the same year.

'Whisky In The Jar' (Traditional arr. Lynott, Bell, Downey, full-length version 5:45)

Released as a cut-down 3:43 single on 3 November 1972, intended as the B-side to 'Black Boys On The Corner' but then promoted to be the A-side before release, this was the song that gave Thin Lizzy their first taste of chart success. This single is almost worth a chapter of its own; it gave the band the leg-up they required and effectively saved their careers (for the first time) and their sanity. The story behind it is not a short one either.

Firstly though, a word about the spelling: Scotch distillers invariably describe their wares as 'whisky', without an 'e'. Most Irish and American brands are labelled as 'whiskey' with an 'e'. When referred to in print, the name of this single is almost inevitably spelt with an 'e', which would be the correct spelling – however, neither on the original single nor on any subsequent canonical release, did it ever contain the 'e'.

After Lizzy's first two albums bombed, they were starting to lose heart and their record label to lose faith. In line with the mind-set of the day's serious musicians, Thin Lizzy were never about hits or singles; they were a much more album-oriented proposition; in any case, their whimsical, poetry-based, musically complex approach was never likely to churn out the hits like Buddy Holly's simple songs or The Monkees' jolly ditties. Nevertheless, to a record label, a band is just a tool for printing money, and Thin Lizzy needed to come up with a hit single. 'Whisky In The Jar' was never meant to be that single; it is a traditional Irish folk song and the boys started playing it at a jam session one night when they couldn't find inspiration anywhere else. It was their co-manager Ted Carroll who spotted the song's potential in the trio's hands, but clearly, they were trying to come up with something original and wouldn't consider recording the old ballad.

Anyway, Lynott reckoned his new song 'Black Boys On The Corner' was good enough to make the grade; a gritty, funky piece of rock soul, it got the nod from the label. All 45s need a B-side though, and Carroll was keen to promote 'Whisky In The Jar', which played up their Celtic roots nicely, so they reluctantly agreed to hammer out a version.

Clearly, they needed to rock it up a bit, but it reportedly took Eric Bell a fortnight of mucking about, jamming along with a tape copy, before he came up with the now-iconic electric guitar riff that makes Lizzy's version so instantly recognisable. Interestingly, Lynott and Bell both strum acoustic guitars on this one; Eric Bell said they couldn't afford to hire an extra musician, but it never seems to have occurred to them to dub on a bass afterwards, even though they dubbed on the lead guitar – so this song contains no bass guitar.

The single was recorded, pressed and released behind schedule, but despite all the sweat that had gone into it, it too dropped like a stone – at first. Decca had insisted that 'Whisky' would be the featured song out of the two, so it was promoted to the A-side, and some bright spark had the idea of shipping out miniature bottles of whisky to all the DJs and record stations along with copies of the single.

Meanwhile, a demoralised Lizzy were going through the motions on a German tour. Down and depressed, drinking heavily, Lynott and Bell ended up slugging it out in a hotel one night and Downey threatened to pack the whole game in. Then suddenly, they had word from head office that 'Whisky' had hit the charts and was currently residing at no. 25. The tour was a disaster anyway, so they cancelled the rest and high-tailed it back home to promote the single, which eventually climbed to no. 6 in the UK, a massive no. 1 in Ireland, and ironically it ended up getting to no. 10 in Germany too. Amid massive back-slapping and relief all round, it gave Thin Lizzy their first appearance on Top Of The Pops and new kudos with Decca. The big time called.

A word about the song itself: It was based on notorious Irish highwayman Patrick Fleming. Not one of Ireland's finest, he murdered, robbed and maimed indiscriminately, men, women, children, rich and poor alike, and was eventually hunted down and captured. Fleming famously escaped at one point by scrambling up a chimney but was eventually recaptured and was hanged in 1650. It was common for such 'gentlemen of the road' to take on a heroic air in their local district, but in Scotland and Ireland, where they tended to target rich English landlords, they tended to be regarded as national patriots. 'Whisky' was written about the time of Cromwell's invasion of Ireland, when England's repute in Ireland was rock bottom and even a miscreant like Fleming was viewed through rose-coloured glasses. The song was also transferred to America with the Irish emigrants and adapted into various patriotic forms during the Civil War, especially amongst Irish battalions.

If you've ever wondered what that 'Musha ring dumma do dumma da' bit is all about, with its 'whack for ma daddy-o,' the answer is that no-one really knows, as Brian Downey explained to the author:

> Whoever wrote it originally stuck a Gaelic phrase in there, but over the years, the Gaelic was lost and the English was substituted. I mean the song is pretty ancient; 'Highwayman songs' they used to be called. And it was mispronounced over all those years, so it comes out as 'musha ring dumma do dumma da', then it's actually 'whack fol, (with an L), de-daddy-o.'

In any case, after Thin Lizzy went on to success with the Vertigo label, Decca trotted this one out from time to time. The full-length version was released on 27 Jan 1978, with two later songs, 'Vagabonds Of The Western World' and 'Sitamoia' on the B-side. It was then released in 1979 and again in 1983 with 'The Rocker' on the B-side. The single appeared on the Decca compilation *Remembering Part 1* in 1976 and both versions were included on the 2010 expanded 2-CD edition of the album *Vagabonds Of The Western World*.

'Black Boys On the Corner' (Lynott, 3:21)

Released as the B-side to 'Whisky In The Jar' on 3 November 1972, this song showcases Lynott playing up to black stereotypes – the first words are spoken in typical Afro-American tones, with hi-hat and bongos giving it an almost TV Cop show vibe. A percussive, intermittent guitar and bass riff goes for nearly a minute before the band comes in fully, but then the guitar overwhelms the vocals for some reason, in what seems like an appalling mix. There sounds like a groove skip at 1:15, but it's there in all versions, so must be a kind of auditory illusion, unless there is an imperfection in the original pressing. A few rhythm changes and a bluesy slide solo give it a groovy, funk-rock sound, and Lynott sings it in the first person – references to him 'not knowing his place', 'playing his bass' and a stern instruction to 'recognise his face' make the song about him, Phil Lynott, iconoclast and rising rock star. Ignore him at your peril.

'Randolph's Tango' (Lynott, full-length version 3:49)

Released as a non-album single on 4 May 1973 in an edited 2:25 version.
In attempting to ensure that they wouldn't be stereotyped into anything
resembling a folk band, Lynott wrote something as different from 'Whisky' as
he could manage, but really it's just as far in the opposite direction. A sweet
acoustic guitar gives a flamenco flavour to the introduction, but even stranger,
this is really melodic, to the point of being catchy, with a stick rhythm and
an utterly excellent acoustic guitar solo. Is that really Eric Bell? Surely not?
It's a great song in every way (apart from Lynott's insistence on pronouncing
'Randolph' as 'Randalph'), but nothing like any other Thin Lizzy song of any
era. And tragically, even with Thin Lizzy's name now out there in the public's
consciousness, this single still didn't sell. The full-length version was included
in the 1991 CD edition of *Vagabonds,* with both versions eventually being
included on the expanded 2-CD 2010 edition.

'Broken Dreams' (Bell, Downey, Lynott, 4:26)

Released as the B-side to the above single, and in total contrast, a heavy-handed
guitar riff underlies this mid-tempo minor-key 12-bar pub blues. The strange
coil-tapped solo sounds a bit strained next to the beefy humbucker rhythm riff,
with staccato chords contributed by a third guitar. It's a bit weak in all honesty;
a true non-album B-side. For some reason, these four non-album tracks,
released in between *Orphanage and Vagabonds,* are generally included as
bonus tracks on CD versions of *Vagabonds* – but they sit logically here amongst
the *Orphanage* entries.

Vagabonds Of The Western World

Released: UK 21 September 1973, US October 1973
Label: Decca (London in US)
Recorded at: Air Studios and Decca Studios, London, July 1973
Philip Lynott: Vocals, bass guitar, rhythm guitar
Eric Bell: Lead guitar
Brian Downey: Drums, percussion
Kid Jensen: Voice on 'The Hero and the Madman'
Jan Schelhaas: Organ on 'Mama Nature Said' and 'The Hero and the Madman'
Fiachra Trench: String arrangement on 'A Song for While I'm Away'
Produced by: Nick Tauber, Philip Lynott
Album duration: 40 minutes
This album did not chart

Peter Bardon and Brian Tuite had already distanced themselves by the time 'Whisky' was recorded, and a young Scotsman named Chris Morrison had joined forces with Ted Carroll to co-manage the band. 'Whisky' may have given Thin Lizzy a boost and placed them in the public eye, but there's no doubt that it was a one-off for them, almost a novelty single. 'After the success of "Whisky in the Jar" there was an awful lot of pressure on the band,' said Lynott. 'People wanted us to record 'Tipperary' rocked up, or "Danny Boy" rocked up.' Traditional Irish folk tales wasn't where they were at, and it was decided not to put the single on the new album. Lizzy were aiming at higher things.

Nevertheless, without the success of the single, it's by no means certain that the third album would ever have happened, let alone been as good as it was. Without any disrespect to the band's initial efforts, this is such a noticeable step up that the band are almost unrecognisable. The songs are varied, complex and entertaining, the production and mixing are first rate, the album art and packaging are great, and the choice of additional personnel adds a new dimension. A pre-stardom Joan Armatrading is now known to have contributed some uncredited piano work. The 'Cosmic Cowboy' artwork and other-worldly concept raised the band from working-class heroes to artists of note, and optimism reigned.

Sadly though – unbelievably almost – the album, songs, production, concept, artwork, the whole package, tanked again. The boys must have been desperate, wondering what they had to do to break through – it seems to have hit Eric Bell particularly hard, experienced and respected trouper as he was, and he went into a major decline. The boys had never been ones to hold back on the alcohol front and drugs were a regular fixture, but the whole thing went sour for Bell now big time. At a New Year's Eve gig at Queen's University in Belfast, quite a prestigious venue, he was so stoned and plastered he couldn't remember who or what he was and ended up throwing his guitar in the air, kicking the amps over, stumbling offstage and crawling off to sleep in a corner. Lynott and Downey finished the set as a duo. This was taken as Bell's letter of resignation and it was not contested. The next day, Thin Lizzy was still a duo.

Album cover

Lynott knew an artist in Dublin as it happened, who specialised in an imaginative, almost cartoonish comic-book style combining sci-fi and caricature with a colour-rich palette. Jim Fitzpatrick used to design the covers for a music magazine called *Capella,* and Lizzy's tour manager Frank Murray introduced him and Lynott at a pub called Neary's in Dublin. Fitzpatrick would go on to design many of Thin Lizzy's future album covers, starting right here. His comic book-styled design in rich, saturated colours depict the three members of the band looming large over an alien landscape, with streamlined space shuttles (the largest of which was originally based on Eric Bell's 'Lizzymobile' concept), streaking through wisps of blue vapour below a purple sky. The swirly pattern on the stones in the foreground is taken from a stone-age tomb site named Newgrange in the Boyne Valley, County Meath, and a stylised version of Rodney Matthews' cover for the *New Day* EP is also visible. A mutual artist friend named Tim Booth was heavily involved in the design work of some of the albums, and in fact designed the original lettering on this cover, which Fitzpatrick took and incorporated virtually as-is into the final design, which also included details suggested by Lynott, who took a continued personal interest in the work; it was his idea to put a shamrock on the back cover, which has photos of the three band members superimposed on the leaves. Fitzpatrick actually created artwork for a gatefold sleeve, which Decca knocked on the head for financial reasons, sadly. However, he also did a superb poster based on the same style, even more surreal if anything, with purple light beaming from Lynott's eyes.

'Mama Nature Said' (Lynott 4:52)

Now, this is a different animal right from the off. Starting with a screaming slide guitar à la George Thorogood, this is the first Lizzy album to start with a bang. The song itself is structured with pop chords that clash slightly with the overtly bluesy slide, which nevertheless keeps up all the way through, although mixed down when a slide lead solo piles in over the top later on; session man Jan Schelhaas, who would go on to be in the bands Caravan and Camel, contributes keyboards. Key changes abound in a surprisingly complex and musical backing, which underpins a conservation message ahead of its time. According to Mark Putterford's Phil Lynott biography *The Rocker,* it was inspired by a newspaper article that Dennis Keeley, Philomena Lynott's long-time partner, was reading. In any case, this is a green anthem, a lament at what we have done to this world, seen through the eyes of Mama Nature herself – and a long time before it was cool to be green.

'The Hero and the Madman' (Lynott 6:08)

A sprawling, fantasy epic that should have put Thin Lizzy straight into the first division of prog legend, this masterpiece features a spoken narrative by none other than Canadian disc jockey Kid Jensen. His transatlantic accent gives it the feel of a 1950s US drama, although the storyline is difficult to decipher: A heroic fairy-tale figure rides for days to rescue the fair maiden from the tower, but the song interrupts the story as someone asks the hero if he's the one who rocketed into space to search for the lost city of Mars? Suddenly it's not so clear whether he is in fact a hero or a madman, as the watching crowd goad him to climb higher – several storylines knot together as we seem to unmask the hero as an actor that we recognise from several roles. Downey drives the narrative along with a fast hi-hat backing, with bongos and congas going too. Downey plays it all except the congas, which were provided by African percussionist and conductor Kofi Ayivor, although sadly not credited. Lynott voices the madman, but there seem to be several voices on the soundtrack to this movie – from about 3:30 to 4:00 minutes, several massed voices sing harmonies, then as it passes the four-minute mark, we hear from a character called The Wizard, goading our protagonist on as he undertakes his reckless errand. In conversation with the author, Downey insists that there were only two voice performers on this track, Jensen and Lynott, and all the other voices are sped-up or slowed-down versions of Lynott. Bell puts in some serious rock guitar on an extended solo, and once again, Jan Schelhaas plays the organ.

'Slow Blues' (Lynott, Downey 5:14)

The pace dies down now as the boys launch into what would be a stereotypical slow blues, but for the timpanis in the intro! After one verse, though, the moody piece morphs into a funky minor-key 12-bar. An abrupt tempo and chord change at four and a half minutes introduce an almost classical prog section until the timpani brings back another helping of slow blues before the crash ending. It's blues but it ain't; once again the boys defy convention.

'The Rocker' (Lynott, Downey, Bell 5:12)

Released as a single on 9 November 1973 in edited form, 2:41 in length, the first Lizzy album track to be released on 45 rpm. Now this one is a proper rocker and no mistake, with a superb guitar intro and driving bass line. All the poetry is gone; this is pure tough-guy poseur rock, glorying in the life of a swaggering, bar-fighting biker. At the two-minute mark, Bell gets his chains off and unleashes a blistering 2½ minute phase-soaked solo over that driving backing. This might be the only Thin Lizzy song where the original album version is better than the *Live and Dangerous* one. In fact, it is the only Bell-era Lizzy song to make it on to that live set, and as an encore no less. Lizzy's co-manager Ted Carroll gets a little plug for his business here. He ran a vintage record stall in a market off the Portobello Road in London, which later expanded to a second stall in Soho and a third in Camden Town – hence the line, 'I buy my records at the Rock On stall... Teddy boy, you've got them all.' The reference is to Ted Carroll, not directly to the crepe-soled Teddy boy movement of the 1950s. Incidentally, Jim Fitzpatrick did a logo for the rocker, depicting Lynott on a massive, Judge Dredd-styled motor bike – this bike would pop up with various riders from time to time over the course of their catalogue. The song was also released as the B-side to later re-releases of 'Whisky In The Jar'.

'Vagabond Of the Western World' (Lynott 4:44)

How complete a contrast is this? The fantastical Western World of the title is not the western (democratic) bloc as opposed to the eastern (communist) bloc, but a whole mythical land that exists in the far west. The legend of the Vagabond is printed on the inner sleeve, telling the folk-tale of the man who travelled there, his return and the origin of the vagabond race that he sired. This number starts with a folky flavour before morphing into a fusion rocker. It's recognisably Thin Lizzy for large sections; by the end, everything is double-tracked and overdubbed, creating a massive wall of sound. This song saw the light of day again on the B-side of a later release of 'Whisky In The Jar' in 1978, sharing the B-side with the later song 'Sìtamoia'. Please note that the title of the song includes the word 'Vagabond' in the singular, although the album title says 'Vagabonds'. The song is about a person, whereas the album applies the words to the band. Confusing, isn't it?

'Little Girl In Bloom' (Lynott 5:12)

Lynott, the poet, is back, with this atmospherically optimistic ballad. It is generally stated to be based on his own mother, although the girl's life in the song doesn't really match Philomena's. Amp hum and feedback guitar introduce a relaxed, romantic poem over a simple bass line, regarding a young woman, yet to be married but expecting her first child, and anticipating breaking the news to her father. With overdubbed vocals and effects-laden guitars, the boys show they can produce a song with a decent tune, a trick they had only previously pulled on the non-album single 'Randolph's Tango'. Right down to the long, tasteful guitar solo at the end, it's all so simple, but so effective.

'Gonna Creep Up On You' (Lynott, Bell 3:27)

This song has a great start with the dirtiest, sleaziest bass riff imaginable, then a cool wah-wah guitar rhythm that anticipates 'Johnny the Fox'. In fact, this virtually *is* 'Johnny the Fox'. The 'you' at the end of the title phrase is pronounced 'ya,' overdubbed with a breathy syllable, in this coolly ominous but lyrically obscure soul-rock piece.

'A Song For While I'm Away' (Lynott 5:10)

Another gentle and melodic romantic ballad played in a triplet rhythm with lush string arrangements by Irish composer Fiachra Trench, this song reproduces the feel of a 1960s pop piece with chorus and heavily reverbed guitar arpeggios. Trench would reappear later to work with Lynott on his solo recordings. To be honest, this is utterly gorgeous – gentle, calming, romantic and above all, it is another melodic piece. You might even find yourself humming the vocals or the guitar line.

Associated material
'Here I Go Again' (Lynott 4:41)
This non-album track was used as the B-side to 'The Rocker' on its initial release in September 1973. Later editions used the below track. This is an old-time jazz brush swing blues in 3/4, with reverbed slide guitar all the way through, and has nothing to do with the massive Whitesnake hit of the same name. The boys sail on the North Sea before heading for the Big Smoke – Phil name-checks the rest of the band, plus a veritable Uncle-Tom-Cobbleigh-and-all list of characters in the line, 'There was Eric, Brian, Freaky Pete, Charlie, Frankie Lee and me.' Eric, Brian and 'me' are the band of course; 'Freaky' Pete Eustace was the band's roadie and sound engineer from just outside London, although he settled in Galway, Ireland for some years in the 1960s. He also gets a mention in the sleeve notes to the later *Jailbreak* album. Frank Murray was the band's Road Manager and a long-term friend of Lynott's; for some reason, Lynott refers to him here as Frankie Lee. That just leaves Charlie; the band had a driver named 'Big' Charlie MacLennan who played a role in getting Brian Robertson into the band a little later on, but this mention appears to reference Charlie MacPherson, another member of the crew.

'A Ride In The Lizzy Mobile' (Bell 4:07)
This non-album track was used as the B-side to 'The Rocker' on later releases of the single. A slice of pure southern boogie in which Eric Bell gives his only recorded vocal performance with the band, sharing the lead vocals with Lynott. Brian Downey credits Bell in conversation with the author:

> That's Eric! The contrast is really pretty stark, but it sounds effective, you know? I wasn't really sure at the time; I wasn't really 100% into it at the time for some reason – oh man, Phil's not singing the whole song, what's going on? It's disaster time. But actually, after listening to it a few times, I'm used to it and it sounds OK now. It was the only time that Eric got a chance to sing on any Thin Lizzy record, and it was only half a vocal!

He needn't have worried; Eric's voice sounds great on this; his guitar tone is a bit thin and wimpy, but he plays some great Lynyrd Skynyrd riffage. Driving a car in the rain is used as a metaphor for life; the car is never called the Lizzy Mobile in the song, but the mobile should be pronounced 'mobil', and it probably should have been one word as in 'Batmobile'. In fact, the song turns up on various rarities compilations and remastered pressings as 'Cruising In The Lizzymobile'; it appeared under this title on the 2010 expanded 2-CD edition of *Vagabonds*.

'Little Darling' (Lynott 2:55)
Released as a single on 11 April 1974, this is the first Thin Lizzy song to be released with Gary Moore on guitar. Much heavier than we are used to at this

vintage, a riff-driven guitar backing is played on an unusual sound, which seems almost trumpet-like until a real horn section comes in halfway through. A wah-wah slide solo is followed by a conventional guitar solo that doesn't want to stop; Moore screams a repetitive riff all over the last verse. The lyrics are basic I'm-gonna-love-you-tonight fare. Decca included it on their 1976 compilation *Remembering Part 1* and it also turned up on the 2010 2-CD release of *Vagabonds*.

'Sìtamoia' (Downey 3:20)

You may love this or hate it, but this is undoubtedly unlike anything else you have ever heard. The writer's credit is usually (but not always) attributed to Downey, making it the only Lizzy song to carry his name as the sole writer, although there is a story that Lynott gave Downey the writer's credit as a present. In conversation with the author, Downey himself credited Lynott with the words, at least the English-spoken sections. The song launches in with Downey playing a fast and intense tribal beat that does not ease up for a moment, while Moore and Lynott jam round it. There is an English lyric line bemoaning the vulnerability of the poor abandoned children in the cold, seemingly referring to Ethiopian refugees, while stating 'My heart belongs to Glasgow', which references Will Fyffe's 1920 music hall hit, 'I Belong To Glasgow'. The title is pronounced something like 'Shitta-MO-wee-ya' using English phonetics, with the emphasis on the middle 'mo'. According to Brian Downey, it translates into English approximately as 'My old mother, the hag with the money.'

The message is confusing, if there is any message at all, but the music is powerful; a gipsy violin drops in and out of the mix and Moore contributes an incongruous double-tracked Celtic rock solo that foreshadows sections from 'Black Rose'. In fact, during the development of the song, Moore used to play a fast instrumental extract from traditional song 'The Mason's Apron' in the middle, but he didn't include it when the track was finally recorded. 'It suited Sìtamoia perfectly,' says Downey, 'but when it came to recording, he didn't use it. He kept it for some reason; he used something else, and then he used "The Mason's Apron" when he came back into the band some years later.' The extract eventually surfaced as part of 'Róisín Dubh (Black Rose)'. Sìtamoia never saw the light of day until Decca's 1977 compilation *Remembering Part 1*, although Lizzy played a version for the *John Peel Sessions* on Radio 1 in 1974, with Robertson and Gorham presenting a tighter, twin-guitar-based rhythm. It was subsequently given another airing on the reverse of a later release of 'Whisky In The Jar' in 1978, sharing the B-side with 'Vagabond Of The Western World', and also turned up on the 2010 2-CD release of *Vagabonds*.

Nightlife

Released: UK 8 November 1974, also released in US
Label: Vertigo
Recorded at: Saturn Studios, Worthing, UK, April 1974; Trident Studios and
Olympic Studios, London, UK, September 1974
Brian Robertson: Guitar
Brian Downey: Drums and percussion
Phil Lynott: Bass, vocals, guitar
Scott Gorham: Guitar, vocals
Frankie Miller: Vocals on 'Still In Love With You'
Gary Moore: Guitar on 'Still In Love With You'
Jimmy Horowitz: String arrangements (spelt Horrowitz on the album)
Jean Roussel: Keyboards (spelt Roussell on the album)
Produced by: Ron Nevison and Phil Lynott
Album duration: 37 minutes
This album did not chart

First things first, let's get the album title sorted out – it is *Nightlife,* one word.
However, the title track, 'Night Life', is written as two words on all authoritative
editions of the album.

Old compadre Gary Moore stepped in to fill Bell's shoes on the remainder
of the *Vagabonds* tour and remained for a few months, even doing some
recording with the band. Decca had decided not to renew their contract; they
still had one single left to do, and Moore played on the 'Little Darling' 45,
which also sank without trace, as well as doing some preliminary recordings
for a new album. He wasn't fully committed to Thin Lizzy though; he had
already released an album named *Grinding Stone* with his own Gary Moore
Band in 1973, and Lizzy didn't interest him as much as some other things
he wanted to do. In fact, he was keen to get out before being tied down
contractually. When he handed in his notice in the Spring of 1974, Lynott
elected to expand the band to a 4-piece with two lead guitarists, a format
that was putting Wishbone Ash in the forefront of prog and rock at the time.
The break with the power trio format was also accompanied by a complete
change of direction, as the proggy, complex and poetical elements are almost
all gone. In truth, it's a different band altogether, and seeing as Lynott and
Downey had played together in the Black Eagles and Orphanage before
founding Thin Lizzy, there was due precedent for changing the band name
and starting afresh with the new twin-guitar sound. However, whatever
momentum and goodwill they had managed to build previously would have
to be sacrificed and there was no guarantee that any other labels would be
interested in a completely unknown name, so Thin Lizzy it remained. Gary
Moore joined drummer John Hiseman's new incarnation of fusion jam band
Colosseum, imaginatively named Colosseum II.

Ex-Atomic Rooster guitarist John Cann (later known as John Du Cann), then playing with the aforementioned Purple Records outfit Hard Stuff, was recruited by Thin Lizzy and paired with German guitarist Andy Gee for a tour of Germany in 1974, but it was only ever going to be temporary. Gee was contractually committed to another label, and reportedly, Lynott and Cann didn't get on; by the end of the tour, a disillusioned Downey had decided to quit.

Lynott managed to bring him round, but it was clear to both of them that a change was needed. Still persevering with the Thin Lizzy name, they auditioned for replacement guitarists and settled almost immediately on teenaged Scot Brian Robertson. He had been a massive fan of the old Lizzy and had previously met and impressed Downey with his knowledge of their set after a gig in Glasgow. Californian Gorham, on the other hand, was a last-minute signing, turning up right at the end of auditions when Lynott and Downey had almost lost hope of finding anyone suitable. Robertson, dubbed 'Robbo' to avoid confusion with Brian Downey, was a hot-tempered whizz-kid who wore his emotions on his sleeve; he and Lynott would consistently rub each other up the wrong way in years to come. Gorham, on the other hand, would go on to become a cornerstone of the band for the rest of its existence. A bit of a reshuffle was taking place in their management; Ted Carroll quit, citing Lynott and Robertson's head-to-head animosity as a contributory cause, although Chris O'Donnell and Chris Morrison seemed to be holding things together. As it happens, Phonogram had launched their Vertigo subsidiary in 1969 with a specific brief to promote progressive rock and other styles that were outside the pop mainstream, and virtually with his last gasp as a Thin Lizzy exec, Ted Carroll had put one of the Phonogram guys on to the band. A couple of other labels had taken a sniff but turned their noses up, but after a specially-staged gig at the Marquee in London, Phonogram offered them a deal. They recorded *Nightlife* as a 4-piece under the auspices of producer Ron Nevison – and as so often happens, a change of label accompanied a major shift in the musical trajectory of the band.

The album tends to polarise opinion; some feel it is a weak and tentative step towards what the band would later become, while others see it as a lost, underplayed and underrated classic. This writer stands firmly with the former group: this is definitely a poor relation, sitting as a kind of watershed between the fully-developed prog masterpiece that was *Vagabonds,* and the triumphantly melodious pop-rock sound that would define the classic era to come. The guitars are weak and scratchy; their harmonies stubbornly refuse to gel; the mix is patchy and the songs generally weak. That's not to say there isn't some good stuff on here, but it's heavily disguised. It was Robertson and Gorham's first go at professional music, and their first album; looking back, they both criticise Nevison's flash-Harry posturing, lack of engagement and generally casual treatment of their new venture. A bevvy of guest musicians was recruited, including a string arranger, but it was the same old story – like all of its predecessors, *Nightlife* sank like a stone.

Album cover

Jim Fitzpatrick was brought back to design another cover, and this spectacular piece of urban fantasy is one of the coolest things he's ever done. A sprawling night-time metropolis of skyscrapers spreads into the distance, with clear tracks of headlights on the highways as if taken with a long camera exposure. You can almost hear the rumble of distant traffic and the wail of police sirens as an unnaturally large moon rises against a livid sky. In the foreground, a black panther crouches warily on a rocky outcrop high above the scene. The band name and album title are picked out in complex script, very Roger Dean, although Fitzpatrick also designed an angular, more geometric design for the band name, which is used on the back cover underneath a cool studio photo of the band. This logo would go on to become the most familiar depiction of the Thin Lizzy brand. Fitzpatrick explains the rationale behind the cover, constructed in collaboration with Lynott, on his own website *jimfitzpatrick.com:*

> The sullen, moody, almost threatening cover was intended as an almost subliminal political statement, but we dared not say so… The black panther was a silent tribute by both of us to great African Americans like Martin Luther King, Malcolm X, Bobby Smith, and John Carlos, Black Power and the Black Panther movement. We would have had a real job of explaining that one to the record company!

'She Knows' (Lynott, Gorham 5:13)

Lynott refers once again to his Catholic roots for this funky soul-pop with a religious twist venerating the Virgin Mary, who is apparently willing to give the funk and the junk when you're in need of a fix. It is completely unlike anything they have ever done before, groovy and head-bobbingly rhythmic with power chords, but not too powerful. There is a lightweight lead guitar noodling away under the choruses; an Allman Brothers-style harmony guitar solo is followed by two separate ones from the two new lads. Several bridges add a bit of musical originality, with a harmony riff at the end that doesn't really gel in the way we later come to expect.

'Night Life' (Lynott 3:55)

This starts off as pure blues for the intro and one verse, in which Lynott sings a vocal line that he has quite clearly appropriated directly from the 1963 Willie Nelson jazz-blues song of the same name. Lizzy's version is a different song after that, morphing into a funky, soulful 12-bar, while still using Nelson's lyrics as a hook line in the chorus. It is worth remembering that the wholesale 'borrowing' of sections of older songs was quite common practice in the '70s – in fact, Led Zeppelin became famous for it – but especially with blues, which tends to be a very fixed format, the lyrics were shared around quite extensively. The reference to Nelson's song, therefore, takes the form more of an *homage* than plagiarism; nevertheless, it seems a bit of a stretch to list Lynott as the sole writer for this number, with Nelson not even getting a nod anywhere on the album cover. The string section that comes in at about two and a half minutes is somewhat unexpected in such a bluesy piece, but it's not without precedent; 'Need Your Love So Bad' by Peter Green's Fleetwood Mac comes to mind. The mix of bluesy rock and heavy strings anticipates the later sounds of ELO to some extent and works surprisingly well; the theme of someone being completely at home in the sleazy underworld of the city ties in beautifully with the urban panther on the sleeve. This song was released as the B-side to the Germany-only single 'It's Only Money' and the US-only single 'Showdown'.

'It's Only Money' (Lynott 2:47)
A hard-rocking mid-tempo intro stops abruptly for Lynott to half-sing, half speak some fast vocals over a solid drum beat. It's as much rap as anything else, and thus once more Lynott shows himself ahead of his time. More kind of pseudo-religious imagery is mixed in with gritty urban images of people desperate enough to do anything for money. This song was released as a single in Germany only, with 'Night Life' on the B-side, and Brian Robertson also covered it on his solo album *Diamonds And Dirt* in 2011. A demo version exists with guitar work by Gary Moore, which is included on the 2012 expanded 2-CD edition of the album.

'Still In Love With You' (Lynott 5:40)
This tear-jerking torch ballad is the only song on the album to survive from Gary Moore's brief tenure, recorded at Saturn Sound Studios in Worthing, West Sussex. Moore maintained that some of the source material for this song was contributed by a number he was working on named 'I'll Help You See It Through', although he is not given a writer's credit. Nevertheless, his original solo is retained, and his guitar work on the demo gets much of the credit for impressing Phonogram enough to come and hear them play. The song materialised as Lynott was splitting up with his long-term girlfriend Gale Barber, and it could hardly help but reflect aspects of that relationship. Scots rocker Frankie Miller duets with Lynott on the vocals for some reason. Nowadays it may well be considered cool to have two dudes sharing the vocals on a love song, but seeing as the words are specifically addressed to a woman, whether Gale or otherwise, it just seems a bit odd. This song would go on to be a massive highlight on *Live And Dangerous* later on, with Brian Robertson taking the middle solo, but Moore's end solo here is stunning – and pure Santana in places. It's clear who he had been listening to in his spare time. Frankie Miller, for all his rocking, is only really widely known in the UK for this love ballad and for his daft pop song 'Darlin'' which was a massive hit in 1978, reaching no. 6 in the UK. He was also, inadvertently, the cause of a massive bust-up within the Thin Lizzy ranks, but we shall get to that presently. After Lynott's death in 1986, former Van Morrison collaborator and Humble

Pie member Bobby Tench recorded a cover of this song as a tribute, featuring Robertson on guitar. Tench would go on to front a short-lived reunion of some Lizzy members in 1993, including Downey and Robertson, calling itself The Thin Lizzy Band. British lounge singer Sade also recorded a highly-rated cover of the song in 2011. Incidentally, the band recorded a version for a John Peel radio session in 1974 with Lynott and Moore sharing the vocals, but with totally different lyrics, in which there has been no breakup – just an ongoing declaration of love and support.

'Frankie Carroll' (Lynott, 2:02)
Lynott does write some extremely unpleasant characters, and Frankie Carroll is one of the worst. A really unpleasant poem sung/spoken over completely dry piano arpeggios contributed by Jean Roussel, it tells the story of a wholly unpleasant Irish philanderer and child beater, whose faithful and loving wife does her best to look after him. It's not exactly clear why Lynott named the character after two of his closest buddies, Tour Manager Frank Murray and Co-Manager Ted Carroll, but the song made it onto the album, so we'll assume it was a bit of an in-joke and they all shared a jolly good laugh about it. Massive string arrangements recall the Beatles quite strongly in places, but it's no fun.

'Showdown' (Lynott 4:30)
Released as a US-only single with 'Night Life' on the B-side. For all their rocking pretensions, so far Thin Lizzy have shown themselves at their best with poetry, prog and Irish soul. This is quite possibly the most successful track on the record, as the production lends itself to its funky bass line, groovy drums, followed by wacka-wacka wah guitar, then deep tremolo guitar chords. We have another primitive 'Johnny The Fox' here, featuring a slick and shady character Lynott names as Johnny Cool. The chorus is pure black soul, and once again Lynott shows himself at least as at home in this territory as anywhere else. Girly chorus vocals are prominent under a funky guitar solo at the end. A great, groovy version of the song with quite substantially different lyrics was played on a Bob Harris session for the BBC with the Gary Moore line-up, going into a rocky jam as the song progresses. A demo recording, also with Gary Moore, was included on the 2012 2-CD expanded edition of the album.

'Banshee' (Lynott 1:25)
This is a really short, country-flavoured guitar instrumental with acoustic strumming in 3/4 time. It's not very substantial, but it serves to remind the listener that he or she is listening to a guitar band and to wonder why there are not more instrumentals in the Thin Lizzy catalogue. Lynott left a woebegone love poem named Banshee, which may or may not have been lyrics to fit this music. The Banshee is a phantasmic creature from Irish mythology which heralds death by shrieking or wailing, so it's something

of an incongruous name for this gentle, soothing instrumental, unless it was indeed intended to have lyrics. There are known recordings of vocal versions, but not through official channels, and difficult to track down even via bootlegs.

'Philomena' (Lynott 3:47)
Released as a single on 25 October 1974. A pure Irish rock ballad is sung in broad accent with twangy guitars in the Gaelic style that Scottish pop-rockers Big Country would emulate ten years later. A real throwback to the Eric Bell era, it's interesting that this song, named for and genuinely referencing Phil's mum, was chosen as the sole UK single from the album, another indication that hard rock was not the only possible direction for the band to take. The chorus references the jolly Irish folk song 'Home Boys Home', but the instrumental breaks between the verses are pure classic Lizzy, with harmony guitar work over military snare and probably the first strong example of the short, sharp chord changes that would exemplify the Lizzy sound later on.

'Sha-la-la' (Lynott, Downey 3:23)
Released as the B-side to the above single; up-tempo, very fast and with the heaviest backing on the album by far, Downey pounding away on a double kick-drum the whole way through – nevertheless, the reverb and echo-soaked vocals are mushy and overpowered. That's forgivable though, as there is nothing in the banal, give-me-your-body lyrics worth remembering, but the song does feature some proper Thin Lizzy harmony guitars with heavy soloing. The whole ensemble fades out over a drum solo.

'Dear Heart' (Lynott 4:50)
Fast hi-hat and electric piano lead off another throwback piece in which the vocals are mixed so low as to be barely audible. That's definitely a pity, because Phil the poet is back, with this song and 'Still In Love With You' presenting the best lyrics on the album by far. Lynott bemoans the fate of those who give everything for their dreams and their causes, but end up dead or worse – he seems to reference the 1955 Frank Sinatra film *The Man With The Golden Arm*, in which drugs blight the protagonist's life and a couple of characters go 'over the rail' to their deaths. Towards the end, the Motown strings and chords get everything thrown at them in an attempt at a big album finale, but it doesn't really quite hit the mark; they tried hard with this one to no avail and one wonders why they didn't end on the manic previous track with its enigmatic drum fadeout.

Associated material
'Rock'n'Roll With You' (Lynott 4:48)
Astonishingly, this melodic, rocking, monster of a track didn't make it on to vinyl, despite being a regular fixture in early Gorham/Robertson live shows. It

was performed on one of the 'live-in-the-studio' sets for John Peel's radio show and also made it on to the extensive bootleg compilation *Phil Lynott: The Man And His Music.* Having something of the feelgood rock nature of 'Rosalie' in the performance, it should perhaps have made it on to the next album…

Fighting

Released: UK 12 September 1975, US 1 July 1975
Label: Vertigo
Recorded at: Olympic Studios, London, May 1975
Philip Lynott: Bass guitar, vocals, acoustic guitar
Scott Gorham: Guitar
Brian Robertson: Guitar, backing vocals
Brian Downey: Drums, percussion
Roger Chapman: Backing vocals on 'Rosalie'
Ian McLagan: Piano on 'Rosalie' and 'Silver Dollar'
Produced by: Phil Lynott (uncredited: Keith Harwood)
Album duration: 38 minutes
Chart position: UK: 60

OK, so the experiment with *Nightlife* hadn't been a complete success, but Phonogram hadn't taken the decision to sign them only to toss them straight back in the water at the first setback. In March 1975, Lizzy were booked on a tour of the States for the first time, supporting some big names up and down the country for six weeks. Too big for their boots by far, the undisciplined Irish troupe were given a right royal kick up the backside by the professionals they were now working with: compared to ZZ Top, Bob Seger and Bachman Turner Overdrive, they were rank amateurs, but they were nothing if not fast learners and they tightened up their act in a hurry. By the time they returned from the States, they were regularly upstaging their mentors; they had graduated from finishing school and took to touring back in the UK with a renewed enthusiasm and some genuine star quality. They recorded their fifth album in the summer of that year, and the transformation was astounding. *Fighting* has subtlety and variety, but the whimsical poetry and the funky soul had been jettisoned in favour of an altogether harder image, rammed home by a defiantly aggressive front cover that presented the boys as a tough, urban street gang. Perhaps most tellingly of all, Phil rolled up his sleeves and handled production duties himself, abetted by Keith Harwood, who had been an assistant Producer on *Nightlife,* and the sound sprang to life in their hands. In fact, the unthinkable happened, and the album actually made a showing in the charts, even though every one of Lizzy's instantly recognisable classics (with the exception of 'Whisky In The Jar'), was yet to come – still invisible in the States, nevertheless *Fighting* hit no. 60 in the UK and also made a respectable showing at no. 49 on the Swedish chart.

Furthermore, although the label had nixed another cover by Jim Fitzpatrick, they appropriated his angular Thin Lizzy logo from the back of *Nightlife* and used it on the front cover of *Fighting*. But let's be plain here – although *Fighting* is a rock album, it isn't heavy, except in patches. Mostly it is melodic and soulful, whatever the tough-guy sleeve design may imply.

Album cover

The record label had some idea of projecting an altogether tougher image of the band than the whimsical drawings of Jim Fitzpatrick implied, and packed the boys off to the back streets of London with a brace of photographers. The camera angle is at ground level, facing up at the boys looming menacingly over the viewer. The band are lightly armed, but only Brian Robertson looks like he means business, pulling a face that would crack a mirror at 100 yards. A similar shot is used on the back, although the band look more casual and less threatening, leaning against a brick wall – you'd probably still walk by on the other side of the street though. It looks like the same photoshoot, although the guys are wearing different clothes; the front photo is credited to Paul Anthony and the back to Mick Rock. Notwithstanding the photographers' evident skills, (and they are decent shots to be honest), the band have come out pretty unanimously deriding the design as probably the worst album cover in history. To be honest, although it's not a classic, there have been a lot worse. The US version is arguably worse for instance; another grimy brick backdrop, another photoshoot, but this time with the band pouting at the camera like chorus line pinups. Another unused concept had the foursome in close-up, with bloodied noses and cut lips, as if in the aftermath of an actual rumble, but this was taken to be a step too far.

'Rosalie' (Bob Seger 3:11)

Released on 27 June 1975 as the album's lead single, except in Greece, where it was relegated to the B-side of 'Wild One'. A rumbling, constant bass note underpins this rocking version of the Bob Seger number. Although it is cool and classy rather than overly hard or heavy, it is still definitely rocked-up over Seger's country-boogie original, powerful and assured, with backing vocals mixed to perfection and a perfectly-executed wah guitar solo. Seger released the song on his 1973 album *Back In '72*, about Rosalie Trombley who was Music Director at CKLW, an AM radio station in Windsor Ontario, just across the US/Canada border from Detroit – that's why 'She's got the power – she's got the tower.' Although it sounds like a full-on, admiring ode to some lovely Rosalie, Seger is said to have written it as a bit of a moan about Trombley's reluctance to play music from his then-current albums – hence the line "She makes the choices, then you best be smiling when it's choosing time." This version featured guest spots from a couple of high-profile musicians, but they go almost unremarked in the mix – Ian McLagan from The Small Faces contributes piano, and the great Roger Chapman, frontman from Family, does backing vocals. The only time Chapman's utterly distinctive gruff warble shines though is in the 'Yeeeaaaah' at 1:52. If you get the bins on, though, he is powering away all the way through, albeit surreptitiously low in the mix.

'For Those Who Love To Live' (Downey, Lynott 3:08)

Released as the B-side to 'Wild One' in the UK, this is a faster number, but in lighter, melodic light rock territory. Lynott, a lifelong Manchester United fan, often introduced this number at gigs as being written for Northern Irish international footballer George Best, who you may remember, used to drink at Philomena's hotel in Manchester. Best was no stranger to the tabloids, his tempestuous private life often eclipsing his footballing headlines, which was no mean feat for one of the greatest sportsmen alive. After a strident harmony guitar intro it switches down a gear and Gorham plays an ambient riff, and although that sweet guitar backing on this rendition is a bit too loud and the vocals are a bit too quiet, the whole sound is so tight and professional that it's clear Lizzy have taken another great step forward. Strident harmony guitars hit hard at a minute and a half, gelling much better than on the previous album; the band really sounds like a proper unit. The whole solo is thought out and harmonic, progressing into a heavier section at the end with everyone going flat out, no rhythm guitars at this point, then a lovely tight ending.

'Suicide' (Lynott 5:12)
Developed from a song from the Eric Bell era named 'Baby's Been Messing', which never made it on to an album, the number had been around since '71 or '72. A character named Peter Brent is specifically named, because the lyrics are based on the plot of an April 1963 episode of US detective show *Perry Mason*. In the show, Brent's partner develops an elaborate fraud involving his own fake suicide, but when he winds up dead for real, Brent is accused of his murder... Lynott identifies the police case in the song as 'number 81', which in fact was the number of the bus he used to ride! A masterful composition, the key rises at 2:30, then Robertson launches into a wah solo that really rocks. Gorham takes the second solo, which is more tasteful and clearer-toned, panning across the speakers at the end, before the two guitars go into a cross-rhythmed 8-bar break, beautifully executed. Up-tempo and heavy, with a rocking guitar riff and solid, rumbling bass, the song is dominated by swinging, rocking guitars, which add up to a seriously epic track – even if the ending is a bit feeble.

'Wild One' (Lynott 4:18)
Released as a single on 17 October 1975. Back to melodic pop-rock here, but the sensitive drumming grooves it along. That's Lynott playing the acoustic guitar. The song comes across as a desolate plea from loving parents to their children, to stay safe at least, even if they never return home 'to those who love and made' them, although Lynott explained that the singer is actually Ireland itself, calling to its absent children as it were. The harmony guitar solo is just brilliant, tuneful and tasteful; you can almost hear the guys grinning at each other in self-satisfied delight at the sweet tones. It's West Coast borderline country in fact; easy to imagine the Eagles playing. Fittingly, this one finishes on a rising, reverb-soaked, harmony guitar riff.

'Fighting My Way Back' (Lynott 3:12)
We are back to the cop-show funk here, with an intermittent power chord intro and quiet wah guitar twinkling underneath. Lynott is up-front and aggressive,

with a defiant laugh in his voice at the same time. This could definitely be an anthem for the band at this time, given the savage beating they had taken so far. Gorham plays a solo with chorus or phasing on it, mixed a bit low for some reason, but there is a wicked, tight ending.

'King's Vengeance' (Gorham, Lynott 4:08)

A fan favourite, this one wasn't supposed to be on the album at all, and was written after the first draft recording had been submitted to the suits at Vertigo – they pulled a number of songs and told Phil to go and write some more to replace them, and this is one of the second-generation results. It starts with light guitar before going into a rhythmic, groovy soul-rock song. It's very musical and quite complex, but the vocals and solo get a bit lost in the mix. There is a bit of a weird high vocal ending, fading straight into the next song on a thunderclap over long echo.

'Spirit Slips Away' (Lynott 4:35)

This ambient ballad features slow, ominous chords over tight, fast hi-hat, with clear-toned guitar chords that underlie a ballad about death. A Robertson solo melds with harmonising feedback solo notes underneath; the ambience is enhanced by twittering sound effects at intervals, fading out over a howling wind. It's all a bit Gothic.

'Silver Dollar' (Robertson 3:26)

This one seems to draw a lot of criticism, possibly over its country-rock fingerstyle intro. For the life of me, I can't see why though; it's groovy country rock with a great opening riff, and Robertson's lyrics regarding a woman's leaning towards unfaithfulness seem legit enough. It pauses at 2:30 before Robertson launches into a solo with subtle piano-work from Ian McLagan underneath. OK, maybe it kind of peters out a bit at the end, but it's a real head-bobber – an instrumental take named 'Bryan's Funky Fazer' (complete with that spelling of Brian Robertson's first name) appears on the deluxe 2-CD version. Incidentally, this is only the second recorded Thin Lizzy song not to have Lynott's name on the writer's credits – the first was Eric Bell's Ray-Gun on the first album.

'Freedom Song' (Gorham, Lynott 3:32)

This is another melodic ballad, this time about a certain Jack Macduff who is lynched by a mob in response to his fight for freedom. It's a pretty grim story, but played in an upbeat, major key style – it brings to mind southern States black oppression, but although McDuff cannot be traced to any real person, the naming convention is conspicuously Celtic. It must have resonated with some in the States though, as this song replaced 'For Those Who Love To Live' as the US and Canadian B-side to 'Wild One'. Some more carefully thought-out harmony guitars, with tasteful bits thrown in and a jolly, laid-back solo.

'Ballad Of A Hard Man' (Gorham 3:14)
Strangely enough, this is the third and last canonical Thin Lizzy album cut to be written by someone in the band yet not to have Lynott on the writer's credits. A hard rock guitar riff opens an aggressive, repetitive piece played mainly in 10/8 – that is to say, an extra two beats are added every couple of bars. There is a rap vocal section with phrases coming alternately from each channel, and definite shades of 'The Rocker' in the gritty, unpleasant lyrics. Possibly the heaviest thing on the album, except for 'Suicide' maybe, if not necessarily the best – it seems like something of a lost opportunity as the promising riff doesn't end up going anywhere and the solo is largely overpowered by the back rhythm. The album fade-out after the solo is a bit of an anti-climax, to be honest, but then it follows the example of several of the individual tracks that peter out at the end.

Associated material
'Half Caste' (Lynott 3:39)
Released as the B-side to 'Rosalie', this non-album oddity starts on solo bass, before settling into a gentle calypso rhythm, relaxed and gentle, despite the hard-edged lyric, which describes casual racism. The mixed-parentage boy in the song could obviously be Lynott himself, but there is no record that Phil was ever victimised like our hero who gets it from both sides. The tropical vibe is certainly a bit leftfield for Thin Lizzy, but it's also superbly executed. A clear-toned guitar solo is offered over wah-wah strumming, before a lengthy fadeout. The song pulled double-duty in the *Johnny The Fox* era, as B-side to the US/Canada/Australia single release of 'Rocky'.

'Try A Little Harder' (Lynott, Robertson 4:08)
The Holy Ghost gets a rare mention in this non-album minor-key ballad with slow tremolo on the backing chords. The reverb-soaked solo is melodic and tasteful, with a lyric concerning a man resolving to be a better witness to his religious ideals, which may be one reason why it was essentially buried despite being a master-class in musicality; the two rhythm guitars play cross-rhythms that gel superbly. The arrangement gets ever so gradually more intense and even starts to sound as if it is speeding up, which is an aural illusion. A remarkable series of complex key changes towards the end make it a seriously musical piece. Sadly, it never saw daylight until the 2001 4-CD retrospective *Vagabonds Kings Warriors Angels*, but was later included on the 2012 2-CD expanded version of *Fighting*.

'Song For Jesse' (Lynott 2:14)
This non-album demo consists mainly of acoustic guitar chords underneath a twinkly piano with occasional vocalisations; Robbo is playing the piano. The basis of a potentially beautiful track that never materialised, it was included on the 2012 deluxe 2-CD edition of the album.

'Leaving Town' (Lynott 5:52)

The timing given here is from the instrumental version on the 2012 deluxe 2-CD edition of *Fighting*, but there are several versions of different lengths kicking around, some with vocals. The song is a late-night, downbeat and morose ballad, with a folk-blues feel and mandolin-like guitar. There is some disagreement over its vintage and the line-up too, but the overall feel is of the Robertson/Gorham era.

'Bryan's Funky Fazer' (Robertson 3:38)

An instrumental with this name appears on the 2012 deluxe 2-CD version of *Fighting*, but it is simply an early, pre-vocal take of 'Silver Dollar' – see that song's entry above.

'Blues Boy' (Robertson or Lynott 4:34)

This non-album cut is a real, proper, Chicago slow blues, which deviates slightly from the traditional format towards the end of each verse, resulting in it becoming an 11-bar rather than a 12-bar number. The backing riff is major-key, low-down and sleazy, with two guitars playing harmonising lines. Blues fans will love this, but it may not be every Thin Lizzy fan's cup of tea. Somewhat confusingly, it is included on the 2011/2012 2-CD expanded versions of both *Fighting* and *Jailbreak*, one credited to Robertson as the writer, the other to Lynott.

Jailbreak

Released: UK 26 March 1976, US 18 February 1976
Label: UK Vertigo, US Mercury
Recorded at: Ramport Studios, London, December 1975 – February 1976
Phil Lynott: Bass guitar, acoustic guitar, vocals
Scott Gorham: Lead guitar, guitars
Brian Downey: Drums, percussion
Brian Robertson: Lead guitar, guitars
Tim Hinkley plays keyboards on 'Running Back' but is uncredited on the album notes, as is the unknown sax player on the same track.
Produced by: John Alcock
Album duration: 36 minutes
Chart position: UK: 10, US: 18

Well, *Fighting* had at least sniffed the charts, but it hadn't set them alight, and the two singles it had spawned had both sunk like a stone. This means that out of five albums and all the singles, recorded by various line-ups over a six-year period for two different labels, only 'Whisky In The Jar' had been a major hit – a novelty single, an old Irish ballad that had little or nothing to do with this band of rockers. Thin Lizzy looked like becoming one-hit wonders, and they had cost the label more than they had earned by some considerable margin. The band had a contract with Phonogram for three albums, and they had already had two strikes, so they had to hit the ball this time and hit it hard. They looked outside for a skilled producer once again and came up with John Alcock, who had built a studio in Battersea and had major-league experience with The Who. He was tasked with creating a sonic soundscape that accurately reflected Lizzy's rapidly-rising live reputation, while also being commercially viable. Lynott wrote, Lizzy played and Alcock produced throughout the winter of 1975/76, all the time with Vertigo leaning on them like a ton weight. Alcock did a brilliant job it must be said, but the real taper that lit the touchpaper was a throwaway song Lynott had apparently originally written about soldiers returning from Vietnam. It wouldn't have meant much outside of the USA, but the suits at Vertigo's American subsidiary Mercury were hot for it. The song was reworked, renamed and shoehorned on to the album almost as an afterthought, but it made the boys into rock stars. The album was *Jailbreak*, and the song was 'The Boys Are Back In Town'. Thin Lizzy suddenly started lighting up the US and Canadian charts as well as various places in Europe.

On the vinyl, we find the heaviest power-rock the band has yet produced sitting side-by-side with aching ballads, with some absolutely glorious, tasteful and melodic guitar work underpinned by rock-solid yet sensitive drumming and bass work. The whole set is a bit light at 36 minutes, as were many of the following LPs, but the unit really came together symbiotically for this album, with ideas bouncing around the studio, passages written for one piece being dropped into another, everyone contributing ideas for each other's songs and lots of fine details in the background. No extra instrumentation is credited, although the keyboard washes towards the end of 'Warriors' are an important feature of that number, as is the saxophone on 'Running Back'. The lush gatefold sleeve sci-fi underpinning and short story on the inner sleeve parallel *Vagabonds Of The Western World* and connect this phase of Lizzy's career with the Eric Bell days. *Jailbreak* is a masterpiece, pure and simple, and at last, Thin Lizzy were poised to become international rock stars.

Album cover

Jim Fitzpatrick was reinstated to create the cover art and devised a masterpiece that tied in several themes from the album and elsewhere into a lush and imaginative gatefold sleeve. The inside hosted a trademark comic-book depiction of the foursome on the run, after the theme of the opening title track. The front cover is rendered in a silvery-sheened monochrome, as a grim-faced comic book-style character in the Judge Dredd vein watches the scene play out on his monitor, which is actually a hole in the cover through which we can see the fleeing fugitives. Open up the gatefold to view the picture underneath and we find that the boys are sprinting away, not from the cops or the armed forces, but alien tripods based on H.G. Wells' *War Of The Worlds*. The cyberpunk anti-hero on the cover is at first impression clearly the warrior from the album, watching the jailbreak unfold on his silver screen. Deeper inside the cover though, the plot is muddied by a short story that tells the tale of the jailbreak itself as a noble rebellion, backed by a heroic sword-wielding warrior, against the evil 'Overmaster' of Dimension 5. Suddenly the cover character looks more like the overlord than the ally, and this is confirmed by Fitzpatrick. It doesn't really matter though; the multi-layered theme doesn't so much portray a coherent story as present an atmosphere that represents the band as sci-fi superheroes, determined underdogs out to throw off the yoke of oppression. Incidentally, the hole in the outer cover is only big enough to see three of the band members, but this was not the original intention; in the US edition there is no gatefold, so the hole in the cover lets through to the inner sleeve – the picture inside is correctly shrunk so that a large margin is left around the edge and all four characters can be seen from outside.

'Jailbreak' (Lynott 4:01)

Released as a single 30 July 1976 in the UK (where it reached no. 31) and Ireland, plus Australia where it was titled 'Thin Lizzy's Jailbreak' (to differentiate it from 'AC/DC's Jailbreak'), and the Netherlands. In the US, Canada and most other countries, this track was used as the B-side to 'The Boys Are Back In Town'. So, the set starts with a power chord that can't fail to grab the attention. It rolls into a chunky, tight riff with rock-solid drumming; the bass follows the riff, but mixes so well into the sound it is difficult to pick out individual bass notes. It's not overtly aggressive though; the chords are stabbed, not slammed, and the vocal style is somewhat confidential, almost conspiratorial. Suddenly Lynott shouts 'Breakout!' then alarms and sirens go off as all hell seems to break loose – a last, climbing riff culminating in triumphant harmonising guitar notes, and then the action story continues. The board game Monopoly gets a glancing mention in the line, 'Like the game – if you lose, Go To Jail'. Similar to a number of songs on the previous LP though, this one stops out of the blue on a bit of an anti-climax.

'Angel From The Coast' (Lynott, Robertson 3:03)
A clear-toned funky riff starts this number, with an overdriven cross-riff coming in underneath – it's pure counterpoint; either one of the riffs would have done for the song, but having them both together is genius. As with a number of Lizzy compositions, there are no chords as such; the backing is carried by harmonising riffs. The verses, each of which describes some downbeat, gritty event, are apparently independent of each other as if each one is an individual episode from a TV cop show – the one about a hit-woman who flies in to assassinate a victim then flies out again, provides the title for the song. Despite the content, the song is upbeat and soulful. A harmony solo at a minute and a half precedes a change of key, with yet another funky backing – again, it stops out of nowhere, but at least this time Lynott's last words echo into the distance, as the crook (not Angel, another crook), gets away... then a final pair of chords provide the closing credits. This American-themed, glossy number was chosen as the B-side to 'Cowboy Song', which was only released as a single in the US and Canada.

'Running Back' (Lynott 3:13)
This was the B-side to 'Jailbreak' in the UK and other countries where that track was released as a single. A jolly, buoyant, melodic pop-rock number with a saxophone in the background of all things, shows Lynott's soul-boy side again. A thoughtfully-constructed guitar solo is accompanied by that background saxophone from – who? Not only is the sax player uncredited, but his (or her) identity has completely sunk into the swamp. What we do know is that the jaunty electric piano line that defines this track is provided by session man Tim Hinkley, even though he too is uncredited, and already some grating friction in the band is presaging trouble ahead. The young Robertson was a firebrand without a doubt, a musical prodigy and a loose cannon. He visualised the track in a bluesy vein and played slide guitar on it, as well as laying down a piano track. The management had mooted it as a likely single through, so Lynott wanted it to be chart-friendly and insisted on more of a poppy feel – hence that saxophone and Hinkley's professional presence on the piano. Robbo was incensed and reckons he didn't appear on the final version at all, although the reason has been suggested that he refused point-blank to have anything more to do with it. It's a good pop song no doubt and well produced; some double-claps towards the end come from each side of the pan; a neat extra that it is easy to miss. Lynott's multi-tracked close-harmony singing at the end is a neat trick

too, as the timing is quite demanding. Lynott stated that the song was heavily influenced by Van Morrison, especially his time in the band Them.

'Romeo and the Lonely Girl' (Lynott 3:55)

A whimsical tale of spurned love, this ballad takes the band even further into lightweight pop territory. No wind instruments this time, but this rueful romantic poetry is certainly one of the most melodic pieces Lizzy ever did. Gorham's solo is a masterpiece, clear and plaintive, and mixed decidedly stage-front – it continues underneath the vocal chorus afterwards, moving to the middle of the pan.

'Warriors' (Lynott, Gorham 4:09)

Hell yeah! The band takes a rare detour into fantasy space-rock here, dabbling in prog-metal at the same time, and they utterly nail it. Lynott mumbles a grim apocalyptic tale laced with ominous echo under a complex twin-guitar rock-solid backbeat; Robertson unleashes an utterly superb wah solo as the backing changes completely. A drum-soaked prog conclusion stops short, then the band comes back in with a heavenly chorus over a new riff backed by major 7ths in a keyboard wash. The tight, climactic ending is followed by a few quiet little clicks as the guys can't quite dampen their overwrought guitar strings quick enough. The song is billed as 'Warriors' on the original album sleeve, although the lyrics only tell of one warrior, who serves 'the death machine'. On various compilations and album formats, it appears as 'Warriors', Warrior' or 'The Warrior', but surprisingly, Lynott himself explains the meaning as referring to heavy drug users, who push their physical limits to breaking point in a push for superhuman mental experiences. In an interview at the time with Chris Salewicz of *NME* he said:

> When I wrote 'Warriors' on the Jailbreak album, which is a song about heavy drug-taking, the only way I could give any sense of heavy drug takers was by describing them as warriors; that they actually go out and do it. People like Hendrix and Duane Allman were perfectly aware of the position they were getting into. They weren't slowly being hooked. It was a conscious decision: to go out and take the thing as far as it can go. To the limit. And some of them really did. Tell us what it's like, man.

It seems bizarre because the lyrics don't seem to reference drug use in any way, shape or form. In any case, perhaps with the benefit of hindsight, of all the things these guys might be held in awe for, maybe their pioneering use of addictive chemicals is not the greatest choice.

'The Boys Are Back In Town' (Lynott 4:27)

Released as a single 17 April 1976 in the UK, but not until after it had been a hit in the US. The album's lead single and the first Thin Lizzy single to break into the charts since 'Whisky', it hit no. 8 in the UK and no. 12 in the US. In Ireland, of course, it reached no. 1! Quite probably the most instantly recognisable song in the Lizzy repertoire, it's difficult to see how everyone could have missed its potential, but even getting it on the album was a last-minute decision. The most insistent legend about the song is that Lynott originally wrote it as 'GI Joe Is Back In Town', a consciously US-friendly commentary on the American forces returning from Vietnam.

In fact, though, it went through several iterations with various lyric sets, several amended melody lines and even different themes. It could, however, just as easily apply to any group of nomadic good-timers drifting back into town on a whim; a biker gang maybe, hero-worshipped by the neighbourhood's wide-eyed adolescents; the lyrics are grimily contemporary and distinctly west-coast American. Some of the inspiration was almost certainly taken from the groups that used to congregate in Philomena Lynott's Clifton Grange Hotel, especially the Quality Street Gang, who come more into focus in the next album. In any case, Gorham has gone on record saying that it probably wouldn't have made the final cut were it not for management insistence and the accolades coming from the American distributors. Dino's is the name of a real venue in LA, although not necessarily the kind of dive that would be taken over by boys who 'wanna fight' – it has been suggested that the juke joint in the song was based more on Barney's Beanery, a known hang-out for aspiring rock stars that Thin Lizzy patronised while in LA, or The Rainbow on Sunset Boulevard; or perhaps more likely, Manchester nightclub Deno's. The musical vibe exemplifies the Lizzy quick-change power chord structure, and the loud and clear harmony guitars are a master-class in melodic rock phrasing and climbing harmonies; there is no solo as such, but this cool, rocking classic continues to inspire. After the relatively successful release of the single 'Dedication' in 1991, 'The Boys Are Back' was re-issued, but only climbed to no. 63 in the UK, a creditable no. 16 in Ireland, but sadly nowhere in the US.

'Fight Or Fall' (Lynott 3:45)
A smooth ballad advocating a unified attitude: if we stand as one, we can hold out against those who would beat us down. It could indeed be a call to arms, but it's not presented that way; the calm vibe is more confidential, more a case of hand-on-the-shoulder comradeship. It's easy to assume that Lynott is protesting against racism here, but it sounds more like a trade union speech for higher pay and better working conditions, especially the warning against waiting 'for another year'. The smooth vocals are double-tracked and reverb or echo-laden. Imaginative answer-back vocals are dropped into some extra bars in the middle of one of the verses, just because why not? Gorham supplies another sweetly-considered solo in a heavily reverbed clear Peter Green tone.

'Cowboy Song' (Lynott, Downey 5:16)
Released as a single in the US (where it stalled at no. 77) and Canada only, with 'Angel From The Coast' on the B-side. Lynott returns to his obsession

with the old west, first heard on Lizzy's debut single 'The Farmer'. This classic was written after a US tour, especially Texas, which Lynott absolutely loved. Originally titled 'Derby Blues', when the guys came to lay down the recording, the more prosaic but far more descriptive 'Cowboy Song' came into being. An early live version carrying the name 'Derby Blues' was included on the 2011 2-CD expanded edition of the album. There is actually a harmonica behind those ambient arpeggios at the beginning, abetting the western theme. Another totally classic harmony riff builds from nothing over rising drums, then we hear another brilliant, clear Gorham solo. Loads of modulation on this one as the guys drop in some quiet, calm bits in between hard-rocking solos. Add a few mentions of buffalo, rodeos, busting broncs and a town in Mexico, and the cowboy image is complete. You can almost smell the dust.

'Emerald' (Gorham, Robertson, Downey, Lynott 4:03)
Released as the B-side to 'The Boys Are Back In Town' in the UK, Australia and many other markets; 'Jailbreak' was used instead in several countries including the US and Canada. For the first time since 'The Rocker', Thin Lizzy go out and out on this one, a powerful metal anthem with Gaelic phrasing and a fantasy ambience. Lizzy were not the kind of band to leave things completely to chance; generally, they liked to have some ideas already roughed out before entering the recording studio. In this case, though, the hardest-rocking number on the album was written on the fly in the studio; a grim tale of slaughter and destruction with the aim of overthrowing the overlords and recovering some mythical gemstone – although the green, lush land of Ireland has long been given the epithet 'The Emerald Isle', so maybe it's a power struggle for dominion. On a side note, the song's opening line, "Down from the glen came the marching men, with their shields and their swords," is a dead ringer for The Dubliners' 'McAlpine's Fusiliers': "As down the glen came McAlpine's men, with their shovels slung behind them". The Dubliners' song is a compilation of words drawn from the working songs of Irish Navvies in the 1940s and '50s, labouring for the building corporations on the British mainland; the melody line was based on a song called 'The Foggy Dew'. This tune itself is said to have originated from earlier sources, and so it goes, ad infinitum. For 'Emerald' though, phased guitars, power chords and guitar duelling anticipate 'Black Rose', as an answer-back duet gives way to a hard-rocking, elongated Robertson solo. Awesome! Ends on a single power chord.

Additional material
'Derby Blues' (Lynott, Downey 6:51)
A live cut of this track recorded in 1975 appeared on the 2011 expanded 2-CD edition of *Jailbreak*. Obviously, part of the live set well before *Jailbreak* was recorded, this is simply an early version of the track that would become 'Cowboy Song'. In fact, Lynott introduces it as a new number, 'as yet untitled – we call it Derby Blues.'

Johnny The Fox

Released: UK 16 October 1976, US 15 October 1976
Label: UK Vertigo, US Mercury
Recorded at: Ramport Studios, London, August 1976
Philip Lynott: Bass guitar, acoustic guitar, lead and backing vocals
Brian Downey: Drums and percussion
Scott Gorham: Lead guitar, guitars
Brian Robertson: Lead guitar, guitars
Fiachra Trench: Brass and string arrangements
Phil Collins: Percussion
Kim Beacon: Backing vocals
Produced by: John Alcock
Album duration: 36 minutes
Chart position: UK: 11, US: 52

So how do you follow a triumph like *Jailbreak*? Answer: With a record sleeve, apparently. Jim Fitzpatrick was re-engaged to create a cover for the next album, but without a title to work to, he basically doodled a fantastically complex pattern around the margins, with a mixed flavour of Celtic, Native American and pure fantasy, leaving a small circle in the middle for the actual picture, as soon as anyone should tell him what to put in it.

That the album followed so closely on the heels of *Jailbreak* was due to the kind of misfortune that makes a person curse and shake his fist at the universe. Soon after that album was released, the band were back in the States playing an extended series of support slots for various big rock acts, along with some smaller headline shows. But as 'The Boys Are Back In Town' started making its presence felt in the US charts, Lizzy were booked as support for Ritchie Blackmore's Rainbow on a US tour that could have made them massive. They elected to extend their stay in the US for another month and a half. Their live shows were carving a formidable reputation, they were regularly upstaging the headliners wherever they went, and the opportunity to play to the large audiences Blackmore's crew were commanding was a break that would likely have put them into the rock stratosphere. The boys were celebrating life and partying hard; cocaine was replacing weed and needles started supplementing the booze. On the day of the first Rainbow gig, Lynott's lifestyle caught up with him, he admitted to sharing a needle with another user, ended up hospitalised with a severe case of hepatitis and Lizzy's tour was cancelled. Back at his mother's hotel in Manchester, he slowly recovered, but his sickness had been severe enough at its peak to cause genuine concern. Once he was out of danger, a lot of his enforced leisure time was spent writing the songs for the album that would become *Johnny The Fox*.

When Lynott was well enough, they decamped to Germany to record at Giorgio Moroder's studio in Munich with John Alcock back in the driver's seat. Things didn't work out well in Munich though; there were technical difficulties with the gear, the atmosphere was stark, they were a long way from home and Lynott's constitution had not fully recovered from his brush with death. Soon they were soon back at Alcock's Ramport Studios in Battersea to have a go at recreating the *Jailbreak* magic. To some extent they succeeded; the album is polished and assured and everything falls into place, although surprisingly, the guitar solos are mushed much further down into the mix than they were on *Jailbreak* and almost disappear on some numbers. Genesis drummer (and by now lead vocalist) Phil Collins is credited with added percussion on some of the sessions, but the recollection of which tracks he played on, or whether he appears at all on the final cut, has been lost in the mists of time; similarly with bearded, flat-capped backing vocalist Kim Beacon from Scottish band String Driven Thing.

Whatever would happen with *Johnny The Fox* though, chance had dealt them a cruel blow by denying them the chance to conquer America. Without a tour to hammer home the band's credentials, and with time on their hands, there was pressure to record a new album far sooner than would usually be considered wise. Some great songs had come from behind Lynott's fevered brow, but arguably not enough to fill another top-notch album. *Johnny The Fox* did well in the UK and Europe, but the US was starting to forget about Thin Lizzy already.

The promotional tour for the album produced one of the sources for the band's watershed, career-defining live album, still to come: the climactic Hammersmith Odeon shows in mid-November 1976.

Album cover

Jim Fitzpatrick had been working on the album cover as already mentioned, but because the title still had not been decided upon; all he had was a half-finished album cover design with a big gap in the centre. They toyed with the idea of a warrior figure in there, but it started to get uncomfortably close to the release date before an album title was finalised. An idea to leave it as a hole in *Jailbreak* fashion to reveal a picture of a fox's head underneath was thrown out, but Fitzpatrick's final picture of a skulking fox eyeing a distant metropolis against the backdrop of a massive, rising moon ties in nicely with the design from *Nightlife*. We are not treated to a short story to explain the album title this time, but an extract from the track 'Fool's Gold' is printed on the inner sleeve as a kind of introduction to the fox character.

'Johnny' (Lynott 4:23)

Provisionally titled 'Weasel's Rhapsody', this is a nasty little ditty about a junkie armed robber and murderer. The tight, chunky backing is restrained, but the vocals have a weird kind of short echo that makes them a bit mushy. Once again, Lynott delves into the dark side to tell a narrative story, and there's no happy ending. Robertson's trademark wah solo is clear, but not as pin-sharp as on Jailbreak; the song fades out on another, more extended wah solo, but then inexplicably ends halfway through the fadeout. Note: This is not the same Johnny character from 'Johnny the Fox Meets Jimmy The Weed'. Or is it? Someone named Johnny turns up on most of Thin Lizzy's albums, but this set seems to have more than its fair share. Coincidentally, an Italian-American mobster known as Jimmy 'The Weasel' Frattiano would make headline news the following year by turning States' evidence against the Mafia in 1977.

'Rocky' (Lynott, Gorham, Downey 3:41)
A more aggressive vocal style over more melodic backing with some neat little timing details give this number more of an edge. This ode to a stereotypical rock'n'rollin' guitar-slinger is usually assumed to be about Robbo, which is wholly likely, slick and feisty as he was. The backing riff really rocks, but the solo is so low in the mix as to be totally lost. It has a nice echoing ending, though.

'Borderline' (Lynott, Robertson 4:32)
A slow, end-of-the-evening west coast country ballad in 3/4 time that could easily have come from the Eagles. There is a big, massed vocal chorus, but the mix is a bit strange, and Gorham's solo is completely sunk. Lynott's enforced incarceration while convalescing from hepatitis gave him plenty of time to think and reflect on his life, and this song, ostensibly regarding beer's failure to dispel the despair at another broken love affair, nevertheless implies his recognition that he himself was indeed a borderline case, pushing the boundaries too far for comfort.

'Don't Believe A Word' (Lynott 2:18)
The only UK single on this album, reaching no. 12 in the charts; an up-tempo, pounding live favourite with driving bass, and a harmony guitar backline all the way through – but at less than two and a half minutes, it's over in a flash. Robertson's wah-pedal solo is fantastic, powering the song along between some more grimy lyrics about deliberate deception. The ending is tight and powerful, tugging at the eardrums as the last note quickly fades. It wasn't written as a fast rocker, though. The enduring tale is that Lynott and Robertson really clashed over the original ballad version; Robbo was ever one to say what he thinks, and he reportedly thought the arrangement was appalling, or more probably 'shite'. Downey plays down the conflict, though, explaining the development in gentler terms:

> The original version was slow, and it was one of those numbers we had in line to play. We left it and came back to it a few times, but it wasn't really happening; we had enough slow songs, we didn't need another one. I think it was Brian Robertson who said: 'if that's the case, why don't we just bring the tempo up? Make it just a blues shuffle. Everybody went 'What?? OK, let's try it…' so we tried that.

Robertson and Downey are usually given unofficial credit for developing the rocking version that eventually made it on to the album, but neither were credited as co-writers. The slow version reasserted itself later on. Gary Moore recruited Downey to play drums and Lynott to share the vocals for a tremendous rendition on his 1978 solo album *Back On The Streets,* the same album that gave the world the classic 'Parisienne Walkways', also featuring Lynott and Downey. On his version of 'Don't Believe A Word', Moore plays it slow and soulful for nearly three minutes, producing an absolutely gorgeous solo in the process, then breaks out into a glorious bluesy shuffle for the final minute until it fades out. When Moore appeared on *The Old Grey Whistle Test* rock TV magazine, he was joined on this track by Lynott and Gorham, with Cozy Powell playing the drums and Don Airey on keyboards, but as they couldn't fade out on TV, they finished on a short blast of the Lizzy rock version's riff. This is essentially the version that Lizzy played live when Gary Moore was in the band during the *Black Rose* era and the version that made it to Lizzy's last hurrah on the live album *Life.* But it was taken to another level during the Snowy White years – if you can track down their hour-long radio special *Live At The Hammersmith Odeon* set from November 1981, the slow version gives way to that elongated shuffle section, before morphing into a full-on rendition of Lizzy's original rock version at the end. Downey's judgment is shared by many, when he said, 'I personally thought both versions were good; I thought we could have used either version on the album.' As a side-point, the *Whistle Test* session just mentioned was included on the mega-box-set *Thin Lizzy At The BBC* compilation in 2011, despite not really being a Thin Lizzy session at all, along with the other song they played on that show, Gary Moore's 'Back On The Streets'.

'Fool's Gold' (Lynott 3:51)
This song was released as the B-side to 'Rocky' for the Spanish release of the single. Lynott recites a short poem over heavily reverb-soaked Gaelic backing with an aaah-aaaaah keyboard wash. It stops completely before going into a classic Lizzy pop-rocker with harmony guitars in between the vocal lines in the chorus. This is another product of Lynott's reflections on the shallowness of fame and fortune, chasing the wrong things, money, fame, a transient good time. Oddly though, it seems as if he had two completely different ideas for the song and decided to use them both. He starts off talking about a prospector striking fool's gold in the old west, then we go abruptly into a fairly surreal story about a tightrope ballerina who is saved from a ravening vulture by a super-hero fox… This is the verse that is printed on the inner sleeve.

'Johnny The Fox Meets Jimmy The Weed' (Lynott, Gorham, Downey 3:42)
Released as a US-only single on 30 July 1976, with 'Old Flame' on the B-side. Johnny's sparring partner in this funky soul-filled backstreet anthem is Jimmy

the Weed, which was the nickname of a contemporary real-life Manchester gangster of Irish descent named Jimmy Donnelly. The story is undoubtedly fictionalised and transplanted from the grey streets of Manchester to 'First Street and Main,' and the crooks deal in 'crisp dollar bills' rather than pounds, shillings and pence, but members of the notorious Quality Street gang, including Donnelly, were regulars at the Clifton Grange Hotel at Whalley Range in Manchester and known to (and on friendly terms with) Phil's family. Donnelly even owns the *Johnny The Fox* gold disk that was awarded for a quarter of a million sales and claims it was given to him by Phil himself. There is some contention over why he was known as 'The Weed'; in the song, Lynott states 'he won't use no muscle,' but Donnelly himself was as tough as old boots, fearless in a fight and covered in scars, despite reportedly being notably short in stature. Others say, perhaps with tongue in cheek, that he was called 'The Weed' because he grew on you. The character of Johnny The Fox is a different proposition entirely and is completely fictional as far as anyone knows. Musically, a groovy drum intro leads into a semi-spoken narrative over Starsky and Hutch style funky backing music with some evil wacka-wacka guitar in the background. It's cool, ominous and threatening, but in the song at least, nobody gets hurt.

'Old Flame' (Lynott 3:08)
Lynott drops back into a romantic, whimsical mode with this nostalgic up-tempo and uplifting ballad, reminiscing over an old love. A bit of Robertson's slide guitar lurks in the background, with Gorham contributing a melodic solo. For the US-only single release of 'Johnny The Fox Meets Jimmy The Weed', this lovey-dovey ballad was used as a pretty incongruous B-side.

'Massacre' (Lynott, Gorham, Downey 2:58)
Once again, Lynott attributes this song to his illness, even though the connection is not obvious: a lifelong Catholic, Phil found himself bristling at a visit from a protestant clergyman when in hospital, then afterwards wondered how it could be that religious differences could lead to such ill-feeling. The song is not overtly religious. In fact, it was conceived as a tale of Custer's last stand at the Little Bighorn but the battle described is non-specific. The description of 'Six hundred unknown heroes' that lie dead in the sand, (an exaggeration if it truly is a description of the Little Bighorn), recalls Alfred Lord Tennyson's *The Charge Of The Light Brigade* with its famous refrain, 'Theirs not to make reply, Theirs not to reason why, Theirs but to do and die; Into the valley of Death rode the six hundred.' The link to bigotry and oppression in the name of religion certainly enlightens the song towards the end though: 'If God is in the heavens, how could this happen here? In God's name, they used the weapons for the massacre.' Downey powers the up-tempo rocker along with fast, frenetic drumming, with bongos adding to the breathless pace on the second half of the song, and eerie echo on Lynott's voice. Another super-tight

ending; sounds like they've been working on that.

'Sweet Marie' (Lynott, Gorham 3:55)
This major-7th soaked, wistfully ambient ballad sounds like a Cocteau Twins backing with Lynott crooning tunefully over the top. There is another stringed instrument in the chorus – a dulcimer perhaps? We can hear the west coast again; The Eagles' 'Best Of My Love' comes to mind; there is even some Hank Marvin-style tremolo-arm work in the intro. Robertson's solo is dripping with reverb but still cuts through. A highly musical up-change at 2:30 heralds a slight shift in emphasis as Lynott sings about the pressures of the road – then the connection comes into focus as this is clearly the reason why the lovers are apart. Many commentators see this as filler material in view of Thin Lizzy's burgeoning rock reputation, but it is, without doubt, one of the most melodious, musical and emotionally wrenching love songs the band ever produced.

'Boogie Woogie Dance' (Lynott 3:08)
Mad, frenetic drumming with squealing noises underneath, reminiscent of The Osmonds' rocking 'Crazy Horses', characterise this brow-furrowing oddity – really though, this is pretty horrible. The lyrics are banal, but in Lynott's defence, the only effort he made with them was evidently in sticking his tongue firmly into his cheek. Otherwise, there is simply no excuse for the line, 'In Brazil they got a pill – a real hard power-packed pill – take one too many you'll feel quite ill.' It's all about the fast tempo and tight interludes though; a bit of a wah solo is thrown in towards the end before it mercifully fades out.

Associated material
'Scott's Tune' (Gorham 1:59)
A short place-holder for this undeveloped 12-bar wig-out was recorded during the sessions and later included on the 2011 expanded 2-CD version of the album. It's clearly a straightforward 12-bar jam in which someone has slapped on the tape recorder halfway through, with Gorham wringing some driving rock'n'roll out of his wah pedal, and finishing on a Chuck Berry style riff with a crash ending. Shame it never went anywhere really, it would probably have made a great live track.

Bad Reputation

Released: UK 2 September 1977, also released in US
Label: UK Vertigo, US Mercury
Recorded at: Toronto Sound Studios and Toronto Sounds Interchange, Canada,
May–June 1977
Brian Downey: Drums, percussion
Scott Gorham: Lead guitar, guitars
Philip Lynott: Bass guitar, vocals, string machine, harp
Brian Robertson: Lead guitar, voice box, keyboards
Mary Hopkin-Visconti, Jon Bojic and Ken Morris: Backing vocal on 'Dear Lord'
John Helliwell: Sax and clarinet
Produced by: Tony Visconti
Album duration: 36 minutes
Chart position: UK: 4, US: 39

Johnny The Fox was doing well and Thin Lizzy's star was thankfully still rising.
Once again, a career-boosting US tour beckoned in support of the album,
and the boys were all over it. And once again, fate shoved a stick between the
spokes and the wheels came flying off. One night, Robertson arguably should
have been getting his beauty sleep for the flight the next day, but instead, he
was down the pub with their old mucker Frankie Miller. Miller managed to get
in a fight with the house band and good Glaswegian that he was, Robbo piled
in with fists flying. This was no high-spirited punch-up though; bones were
cracking and broken bottles were being wielded. Robbo managed nobly to
get his hand in between some jagged glass and Miller's face, which no doubt
worked wonders for Miller's view in the mirror ever after, but unfortunately
lacerated Robbo's hand, causing nerve and artery damage. Obviously, he
couldn't play and the tour was once again cancelled, their second US tour to
implode in less than a year. The fiery Scot had been rubbing Lynott up the
wrong way during the recording of the album, and straws and camels being
what they are, Lynott summarily fired Robbo and sank into an alcohol-and-drug-
fuelled depression. Meanwhile, although *Johnny The Fox* did well in Britain and
Ireland, it did not fare so well stateside and the momentum was lost.

A short while later, though, the Lizzy boys went to an album launch for
Queen's new record *A Day At The Races*. Lynott met up with Freddie Mercury,
the two got on like a house on fire, and Thin Lizzy were invited to support
Queen on their upcoming US tour. It was a remarkable stroke of luck despite
the huge chasm in the band left by Robbo and his mangled hand, a gap that
was filled at short notice by Gary Moore. Not only did playing for the mighty
Queen mean bigger audiences than ever before, but both Moore and Lizzy
were at the peak of their powers. Moore was a massive hit with the fans,
and even the somewhat-jaded Gorham was inspired to renewed enthusiasm
and a new lease of life. A master technician, Gorham was keener on the
highly-disciplined dual guitar harmonies than Robertson, who preferred to

exercise his intuitive flair to wing it in the moment. Moore had both; not only unbelievably fleet fingers, but a musical sensibility that insisted on complex and demanding melody lines.

Moore went back to his solo career after the tour, but his tenure had been like a refreshing holiday for the other members of the band, and he would be back soon enough. For now, though, it was time for a new album and the band were taking advantage of a tax loophole by recording outside the UK. American producer Tony Visconti, most famous for collaborating with David Bowie on several of his classic albums as well as with T. Rex, had met Lynott before and had agreed to produce. The band now consisted of Lynott, Downey and Gorham, who was no longer Eric Bell's replacement, no longer Brian Robertson's wingman, no longer second fiddle to the wizard Gary Moore. Suddenly Gorham was in sole charge of the guitar section, he could play what he liked, write whatever harmony lines he liked and double-track them to his heart's content. However, it just wasn't the same. Robertson's hand had healed up and Gorham simply refused to fill all required guitar solos; he deliberately left a few and pressured Lynott to invite the Scot back into the fold. Lynott relented and invited Robbo back, but on a strange, half-cocked basis as a hired gun rather than a full member of the band. Robertson accepted the terms, but with bad grace, turning up to recording sessions, playing a blinder, then grumbling and sulking back into his own world.

This time, personnel troubles notwithstanding, the band were better prepared. The songs were not only written, but rehearsed and more-or-less ready to go, and most drugs were off the menu. Producer Tony Visconti is quoted in *Cowboy Song*, Graeme Thomson's biography of Philip Lynott, as saying that 'When we were in Toronto, the drug of choice was cocaine, which was almost impossible to get. So the band smoked and drank. It was mainly an alcohol-fuelled album.'

Bad Reputation is a strange brew; not only because of the weird personal vibe within the band, but because musically it covered new ground. It hosts some of the band's rockiest, most scintillating arrangements, with complex riffs and off-beat timing, but also a load of soft ballads bordering on country and gospel. It also includes saxophone, clarinet, and some ethereal vocal backings from Visconti's then-wife, Mary Hopkin of 'Once-upon-a-time-there-was-a-tavern', 'Those Were The Days' fame, with assistant engineers Jon Bojic and Ken Morris also chipping in. Strange indeed, as the hardest and rockiest set of their career trails off over the last three songs into anti-climactic, B-side type material. It set the scene though, for the biggest, baddest album of the decade.

Album cover

The packaging is predominantly black, with a stark black and white, high-contrast photo of the trio without Robertson on the front. Fitzpatrick's artwork is notably absent, including the geometric Thin Lizzy logo; instead, the band name and album title are picked out in bold capitals, the band name in white and *Bad Reputation* in red. According to Alan Byrne's book *Thin Lizzy: Soldiers Of Fortune,* Lynott was supposed to meet with Fitzpatrick at the last minute in Madison, Connecticut, but went to Madison, Wisconsin by mistake! There was no time to rectify the problem, hence the rather stripped-down cover design featuring the photo by the Sutton Cooper agency. Robbo was reportedly in full agreement with Lynott's decision to keep him off the cover, still being in a steaming strop over being left out of the band in the first place. Nevertheless, Robbo appears in the casually-posed band photo on the back cover and in the individual photos on the inner sleeve, (although not in another band photo inside), and is listed in the album credits as a full member.

'Soldier of Fortune' (Lynott 5:18)
The album starts with a massive, reverb-soaked gong, then a whooshing synth pad, as Lynott recites a minute-long poem about a mercenary soldier. The whole thing is remarkably upbeat, almost happy-go-lucky despite the killer-for-hire theme, with some pipes or keyboards low under the harmony guitar riff. Strangely, the drumming is a bit stodgy on this one, which may be the first and last time I ever say that about Brian Downey. A nice harmony, echoing riff heralds a false ending before it pauses and starts over, with some military drumming, keyboard washes and sweet guitar, until the main number reasserts itself and builds up to another gong crash at the end. It is a great album starter, without playing all the band's aces in one go.

'Bad Reputation' (Downey, Gorham, Lynott 3:09)
See, the drumming is utterly brilliant on this one, driving the number with its proggy timing, harking back to the early days but much more assured and frankly, better. Gorham wrote the riff, but Lynott and Downey developed the syncopated emphasis that makes it so tight and complex. 'Bad Reputation was one of those songs that came together really quickly' said Gorham, describing how Lynott got the lyrics started. 'As soon as we had that off-timing tag line come in, everything just fell into place, all the harmony guitar work and all that, the lead guitar thing... And he started writing this song called 'Bad Reputation'. This was used as the B-side to the single of 'Dancing In The Moonlight'.

'Opium Trail' (Gorham, Lynott, Downey 3:58)
If anything, this is even more drivingly complex than the previous track, another powerful classic. The lyrics conjure up some surreal images, as Lynott's voice calls and answers from left and right in the mix, confusing and seducing like the drugs of which he sings. According to Phil's biographer Stuart Bailey, this song was inspired by a TV drama on the Chinese organised crime organisations known as the Triads, which had become 'a worrying obsession with Phil'. Lynott and Gorham especially were steadily progressing from weed to cocaine, although Phil's showdown with heroin was still ahead of him.

'Southbound' (Lynott 4:27)

An utterly majestic opening harmony riff is quite quiet, but completely in harmony, almost violinesque. The guitar power chords are heavily overdriven, with a harmonica underneath the guitar solo. The talk of the gold rush and the ghost town tie it to the old west, as does the tumbleweed, although 'chasing my career' makes it sound more like a gig-touring song. This version is simply a pop ballad, not a heartacher the way it comes across on *Live And Dangerous*. The studio gives them more freedom to throw everything at it though, and the ending soars with background harmony guitars, massed harmony vocals and everything else. Glorious!

'Dancing In The Moonlight (It's Caught Me In Its Spotlight)' (Lynott 3:26)

Released as the album's only single in the UK (where it reached no. 14) and Ireland on 29 July 1977. That funky, chunky bass riff with *West Side Story* finger snaps is pure black soul; this pop-rocker with tasty guitar backings may just be the most finely-balanced Lizzy track of all. Without the soaring guitar solo, it would simply be a soul song; John Helliwell from Supertramp even plays sax! That solo though, along with the groovy chord work, balances it on the fence between soul and rock. In this writer's opinion, Gorham plays simply one of the best guitar solos ever, by anyone, before the song fades out on repeated choruses as the bass starts to cut loose a little. The subtitle was added by the band's American record company, Mercury, to distinguish it from the King Harvest song with the same title released four years earlier. Not only is it tuneful, but it even has a catchy chorus.

'Killer Without A Cause' (Gorham/Lynott 3:33)

Another proggily-timed heavy rock riff, this is pure New Wave of British Heavy Metal, not unlike early Iron Maiden. This is until the jolly, upbeat acoustic bridge asserts itself, followed by a high-pitched guitar sounding for all the world like a country and western harmonica. The words conjure up a lone vigilante, a charismatic loner, who comes alive after dark and prowls the streets, foiling crooks and villains. It's very nicely phrased with odd timing features. The hard rock album ends at this point; not that the remainder is particularly poor, but it definitely feels like filler from this point on.

'Downtown Sundown' (Lynott 4:08)

A ballad with surprisingly insistent kick drum which sounds overly heavy-footed. The harmonised vocals present a gospel-oriented theme, with subtle clarinet (yes, clarinet!) from Helliwell noodling away in the background. We are treated to a harmony guitar set piece and a jazzily clear-toned Gorham solo, but apart from that, it is not obviously a Thin Lizzy piece at all. Despite Lynott's lifestyle, which was all about rock and roll excess, he was certainly not shy about presenting his Catholic background as an anchor for the soul.

He sings of a companion that needs her freedom and 'to fly away', but it's all OK because his God will look after him. That, we are told, is the story of the downtown sundown.

'That Woman's Gonna Break Your Heart' (Lynott 3:25)

A big minor-key riff plays over toms that sound more like timpanis with lots of reverb – then suddenly we are into an up-tempo pop ballad. There is a nice echo guitar set-piece with harmony guitars and Robertson is specifically credited on this track. Another melodic pop song with a catchy chorus, it stops suddenly and goes straight into the next song...

'Dear Lord' (Gorham, Lynott 4:26)

Well if we thought 'Downtown Sundown' was a bit gospelly, this one carries the theme further still. A rock intro with heavenly Hopkin choir and phased cymbals leads straight on from the previous piece, with quiet, heavily reverbed lead guitar in the background, reminiscent of Santana's 'Practice What You Preach'. This trails off and the real song fades in over the top, a pleasant gospel ballad, a musical prayer, in which the protagonist is ambivalent between begging for help and saying he doesn't believe a word of it. Big ambient chords with plenty of ambient, soothing 'aaah' vocals work towards a clashing, repeated gong to finish.

Live And Dangerous

Released: UK 2 June 1978, also released in US
Label: UK Vertigo, US Mercury
Recorded at: Hammersmith Odeon, London, UK, 14-16 November 1976;
Seneca College Fieldhouse, Toronto, Canada, 28 October 1977, Tower Theatre,
Pennsylvania, USA, 20-21 October 1977
The band members are not specifically credited on this album, but are
nevertheless:
Philip Lynott: Bass guitar, vocals
Brian Downey: Drums, percussion
Scott Gorham: Lead guitar, backing vocals
Brian Robertson: Lead guitar, backing vocals
The following guest musicians are credited:
Bluesy Huey Lewis: Harmonica (on 'Baby Drives Me Crazy')
John Earle: Saxophone on 'Dancing In The Moonlight'
Produced by: Tony Visconti
Album duration: 77 minutes
Chart position: UK: 2, US: 84

And this is it – the album that put Thin Lizzy into the stratosphere, that
promoted them from rock stars to superstars, from heroes to legends, in
Europe at least. It also, incidentally, converted the image of Thin Lizzy from
a rock band of mid-heaviness to early purveyors of heavy metal. Few other
albums have excited such admiration, even veneration, or such controversy. Its
detractors call it a sham and a fake; its fans call it the best live album in history.
And yet how much of it was actually recorded live is shrouded in mystery and
argument.

The point of a live album is to reproduce the power and excitement of an
actual concert, and the best capture some of the adrenalin and atmosphere
of the night in question. But of course, there is no way to capture on vinyl,
the stab of excitement when you first hear that your heroes will be playing
somewhere near you. There are the months of anticipation; the journey, the
crowds, the gathering of soulmates; the journey to the venue; the sweat and
excitement; the camaraderie or the singalong, fist-pumping volume. If the gig
is captured on vinyl, the recording is more likely to be heard while sitting in
a comfy chair. You might have a cup of tea balanced on the arm, your eyes
closed, headphones on, legs crossed and a tartan slipper dangling lazily from
one toe, while you try to mentally recapture the buzz of the night. In the cold
light of day, every missed beat or screamed off-note can be a source of criticism,
even irritation. So, most live albums, (not all, mind you), are doctored to some
extent in the studio afterwards, faults are rectified, mistakes corrected, spikes
flattened and lulls boosted.

In the wake of *Bad Reputation,* Producer Tony Visconti was in the frame
to engineer a new studio album, but was in such demand that he didn't have

the time. But Lizzy had been recording odd gigs for a while and the results were crying out to be heard, Lizzy did not have a live album in their catalogue and Visconti agreed to create one as a quick fix. *Live And Dangerous* was not even a concert at all. It wasn't all recorded in the same country; not even on the same tour or in the same year, let alone the same night. Cobbled together from two nights at the Hammersmith Odeon on the *Johnny The Fox* tour, and gigs in Toronto and Philadelphia on the *Bad Reputation* tour, it turned out so miraculously coherent that few studio albums can match it for a combination of mix and production quality plus sheer, raw power, spread over 76 minutes and four sides of a double vinyl album. The first of the Hammersmith nights, on 14th November, is widely believed to provide the basis of the album, with contributions from the other gigs mentioned, plus a bit of studio work to bring up the polish. The Philadelphia gigs are not credited on the sleeve at all. Visconti has always maintained that extensive overdubs were added to the recordings afterwards, but members of the band have contradicted this statement with some force. It's a matter of history that Downey didn't redo any of his parts, while both Gorham and Robertson have stated that they did some minor fixes afterwards. However, it is also known that Lynott spent some considerable time at the production sessions with his bass guitar, generally fighting injustice and righting wrongs. How much he overdubbed is a matter of contention, but in any live recording, the drum mics will inevitably register sound from the guitar amps, the amp mics will pick up sound from the bass amp, and the vocal mics will pick up sound from everywhere. Robertson makes the fair point that if you try to overdub one instrument, there will always be ghostly echoes from the original track audible on the tape.

Wherever the truth lies, perhaps no other album before or since so successfully rides that line between hair-prickling, visceral excitement and clear, satisfying production values. It peaked at no. 2 in both the UK and Ireland, but sadly Lizzy's fortunes were already starting to wane in the US, as indicated by the fact that it only crept in at no. 84. Poignantly, this set captured the Gorham/Robertson line-up at its absolute peak, but by the time it was released, Robbo's tenure was already hanging off its hinges and he left the band permanently soon afterwards. It seems that he had already accepted the tenuousness of his position and was making other plans by the time he re-joined Lizzy for the *Bad Reputation* tour, so it was always going to be a temporary arrangement. The timeline starts to get pretty hazy at about this point, but basically, it goes like this: November 1976, the classic Robertson/Gorham line-up of the band recorded the final three nights of the UK *Johnny The Fox* tour, at Hammersmith Odeon. A week or so later, Robertson was injured in a fight and Thin Lizzy had to cancel their US tour. January and February 1977, Lizzy supported Queen on their US tour, with Gary Moore in Robertson's place. May and June 1977, they recorded *Bad Reputation* as an unofficial 3-piece, but Robertson was recalled towards the end as a guest musician. In June, Robertson officially left. In July 1977, he officially re-joined. October 1977, they played the Philadelphia and

Above: An image from the *Thunder and Lightning* tour programme, signed by Phil Lynott after a Portsmouth Guildhall gig in 1983. *(Colin Hunt)*

Left: The self-titled first album, released in 1971. The photo is taken with a fisheye lens at extremely close quarters to the headlight of a rather dilapidated 1950s motor car in an urban street. *(Decca)*

Right: *Shades Of A Blue Orphanage*, 1972. The photograph of the three urchins is a library image. *(Decca)*

Left: *Vagabonds Of The Western World*, the first Thin Lizzy album cover by Jim Fitzpatrick, released in 1973. *(Decca)*

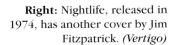

Right: Nightlife, released in 1974, has another cover by Jim Fitzpatrick. *(Vertigo)*

Left: The cover of *Fighting* from 1975, with a photo by Paul Anthony. The CD booklet is signed by Scott Gorham. *(Steve Pilkington)*

Right: The *Jailbreak* cover by Jim Fitzpatrick, released in 1976. This is the original gatefold sleeve, with only three band members visible through the hole in the front cover. *(Vertigo)*

Left: Brian Downey and Eric Bell performing 'Whisky In The Jar' on German TV.

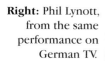

Right: Phil Lynott, from the same performance on German TV.

Left: The famous Thin Lizzy stage logo from a performance of 'Jailbreak' on *Top Of The Pops* in 1976.

Right: Scott Gorham pictured during a live performance of 'That Woman's Gonna Break Your Heart'.

Left: Brian Robertson concentrates from the same live performance.

Right: Phil Lynott emotes, once again during the same live performance of 'That Woman's Gonna Break Your Heart'.

Left: The *Johnny The Fox* cover by Jim Fitzpatrick, released in 1976. *(Vertigo)*

Right: *Bad Reputation*, designed by Sutton Cooper in 1977. Brian Robertson is absent from the cover shot, although he appears on the reverse and in some individual shots on the inner sleeve. *(Vertigo)*

Left: *Live And Dangerous* from 1978, with an absolutely classic photo by Chalkie Davies. How 'rock star' is this? *(Vertigo)*

Right: *Black Rose: A Rock Legend*, with a cover by Jim Fitzpatrick, released in 1979. The album is sub-titled in Irish Gaelic, *Róisín Dubh: Finscéal Cnoc*, on the reverse. *(Vertigo)*

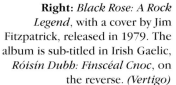

Left: *Chinatown*, with a cover by Jim Fitzpatrick, from 1980. The three-clawed dragon is the symbol of the Chinese Triad crime syndicates. *(Vertigo)*

Right: The *Renegade* cover, with a photo by Graham Hughes, released in 1981. *(Vertigo)*

Left: A still from the video for the cheesy but light-hearted video for 'Sarah' from the hit-strewn *Black Rose*.

Right: The video for 'Do Anything You Want To' from *Black Rose*, which not only features the entire band playing kettle drums, but also four guitars. It all gets amiably silly!

Left: An excellent shot of Brian Downey from the official video for 'Chinatown', released in 1980.

Right: Action shot of Phil Lynott at The Agora, Cleveland, Ohio, USA 1980 on the *Chinatown* Tour. *(Scott Glazier)*

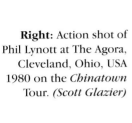

Left: Scott Gorham at Slane Castle in 1981. *(John Crookes)*

Right: Snowy White (left) and Scott Gorham on the Chinatown Tour. *(John Carreiro)*

Left: John Sykes playing live in a televised BBC concert in 1983.

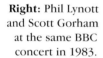

Right: Phil Lynott and Scott Gorham at the same BBC concert in 1983.

Left: Brian Downey, pictured at the BBC in 1983.

Right: Brian Downey relaxing at Folkets Park, Västerås, Sweden in 1983. *(Mats Andersson)*

Left: Phil Lynott backstage, also at Folkets Park, Västerås, Sweden 1983. *(Mats Andersson)*

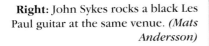

Right: John Sykes rocks a black Les Paul guitar at the same venue. *(Mats Andersson)*

Left: One of Jim Fitzpatrick's art concepts for discussion for *Thunder and Lightning. (Many thanks to Jim Fitzpatrick)*

Above: Another unused concept for *Thunder and Lightning. (Many thanks to Jim Fitzpatrick)*

Right: Unused concept number three for *Thunder and Lightning*. *(Many thanks to Jim Fitzpatrick)*

Left: A fourth untapped seam for *Thunder and Lightning*. Jim says, 'There were about three more substandard ones too in my opinion, including the "fist" image'. *(Many thanks to Jim Fitzpatrick)*

Right: The finished cover for *Thunder And Lightning*, with photography by Bob Elsdale and design by Andrew Prewett, 1983. *(Vertigo)*

Left: *Life (Live)*, the climactic live offering from 1983. A bright blue gatefold sleeve sports a variation of Jim Fitzpatrick's 'Thin Lizzy' logo in huge lettering at the top, with an uncredited photo of Lynott on stage, silhouetted in front of a misty spotlight, underneath. *(Vertigo)*

Right: The *Killers Live EP*, released in 1981. The record was released in seven inch format (nevertheless to be played at 33rpm), with three songs, twelve inch format with four, and also in a Canadian limited edition with six. *(Vertigo)*

Left: Jim Fitzpatrick's art on the reverse of the compilation album *Remembering Part 1*. *(Brian Stroud)*

Above: Scott Gorham performing with Black Star Riders at The Ramblin' Man Fair, Maidstone, Kent in 2017. *(Graeme Stroud)*
Below: Brian Downey performing with Brian Downey's Alive and Dangerous, Nell's Jazz and Blues, London, in 2017. *(Graeme Stroud)*

Above: Work in progress. A portrait of Lynott by Scotty Johnson, unfinished at this point, from an original photo by Fin Costello. *(Scotty Johnson)*

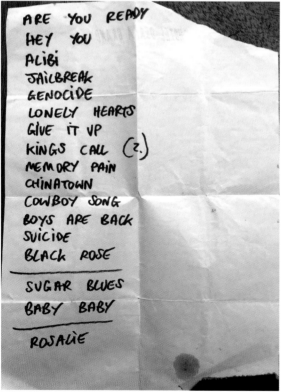

ARE YOU READY
HEY YOU
ALIBI
JAILBREAK
GENOCIDE
LONELY HEARTS
GIVE IT UP
KINGS CALL (2.)
MEMORY PAIN
CHINATOWN
COWBOY SONG
BOYS ARE BACK
SUICIDE
BLACK ROSE

SUGAR BLUES
BABY BABY

ROSALIE

Left: A Handwritten setlist (on the back of Japanese Hotel Osaka Grand stationery) from The Paradise Rock Club, Boston, on the Renegade tour in 1980. *(Mike Mooney)*

Toronto gigs on the *Bad Reputation* tour that would round out the live album. January 1978, *Live And Dangerous* was dubbed and mixed, and released in June. The band was already touring Europe in support of the album, ending the tour towards the end of June. In July 1978, Robertson left for good.

Album Cover

Uninspired as it may seem now, the album was always going to be named *Thin Lizzy Live,* with a gig photo on the front. The change of title was reportedly inspired by a conversation between Lizzy's co-manager Chris O'Donnell and The Clash's Manager Bernard Rhodes. The original idea was to film a video of Thin Lizzy supported by The Clash, which Rhodes turned down on the basis that, 'We are political animals and everything we do has to have an element of danger about it.' Suddenly the name *Live And Dangerous* materialised, the dynamic but unremarkable gig photo was relegated to the back cover, and Chalkie Davies' now-iconic, instantly-recognisable stage-level portrait of Lynott in full flow – leather-trousered, bare-chested, kneeling in front of the lens with Robertson and Gorham outlined in a haze of dry ice behind – became the new front cover. The inside of the gatefold is full of thumbnail gig and studio shots, with more photos of the band adorning the twin inner sleeves. It's an arresting package, worthy of a historic double LP.

'Jailbreak' (from *Jailbreak* 4:44)

Any guitarist will tell you that for sheer firepower, an open 'E' or 'E minor' chord is the best there is. In standard tuning, it uses all six strings, including the lowest note on the guitar, and also the lowest note achievable on a standard 4-string bass. 'E' is the ultimate power chord. So the album fades in with the crowd chanting for 'Lizzy!... Lizzy!...', then the band slams that big 'Em' chord. (The band are tuned a semitone down, so it's actually an E flat – for those that really want to know.) A moment of anticipation, then into that hard, fuzzy riff, with perfectly-executed wah guitar interjections. The restrained, crunchy chords of the studio version are unleashed here as the guys slam their guitars hard; instead of croaking out the vocals in a confidential whisper, Lynott spits them into the mic with barely-controlled aggression. The band still manages to step up a gear at the 'Breakout' bit, and there is still a police siren in there. Already, in the first number, Lynott is interacting with the audience, with his 'We need your helping hands!' The ending is still a bit anticlimactic as per the studio version, but perfectly controlled; there is a moment's pause, then the crowd breaks out into thunderous approval.

'Emerald' (from *Jailbreak* 4:20)

This is a massively powerful number to be played so early in the set! Lynott introduces it with a famous quip about whether anyone had any Irish in them, and whether any of the girls 'would like a little more Irish in them'. A supernaturally fast hi-hat and powerful kick drum make this version even heavier than on the studio album, but the harmony guitar before the solo is perfectly executed. It's clear that Robertson's guitar is coming out of the left channel and Gorham's from the right, but on this occasion, they use radically different guitar sounds. Robertson takes over for the main solo; the bass starts getting a bit freeform, and the whole thing rocks like the blazes. It's an awesome wall of sound with a huge power chord ending.

'Southbound' (from *Bad Reputation* 4:43)

This soaring ballad may seem somewhat out of place in this rocking set, especially leading straight on from the rocking 'Emerald' without any introduction, but the explanation is stranger still: it wasn't in the set at all, not on the *Johnny The Fox* tour anyway. And on the *Bad Reputation* dates, there wasn't a really good rendition to use. Fortunately, they had played it at the soundcheck in Philadelphia, and it was perfect – so Visconti excised the whole song from the live take and dropped the soundcheck version over the top. The crowd applause is therefore genuine; it's just that they were listening to another version of the song. Still, it gives a welcome respite from the breathless rush of 'Emerald' and the ambience is superb, somewhat faster than the studio version, and with perfect backing vocals to boot. At the very end, Downey reaches behind him and strikes a huge gong – he only hits it once during the whole record, and it rounds off the number perfectly as the crowd roars.

'Rosalie'/'Cowgirl Song' (from *Fighting* 4:10)

This live version was released as a single ahead of the album on 28 April 1978 in many countries, reaching no. 20 in the UK, but surprisingly not released in the US – they got 'Cowboy Song' instead. If the sleeve notes of the single are to be believed, this track was actually cut on the 15th November, the second of the three nights. The B-side was a non-album song named 'Me And The Boys', recorded during an encore in Toronto. A brief spoken intro in which Lynott credits Bob Seger, then Robbo launches into that cutting, iconic riff. It's fast and rocky and a bit un-Lizzy like, or would be if this hadn't grown to be the definitive version of the song. Robertson's wah solo is short and succinct, but perfect, and fades into the background at the end. At three minutes, they suddenly stop and roll gently into a laid-back version of the 'Cowboy Song' riff, and the audience claps along as Lynott encourages them. This is one part where the famous studio editing is most blatant. Yes, the crowd were clapping along, but a fault with the forward-facing microphones meant that the recording didn't pick it up properly. So Visconti manufactured his own, taking a sample of applause and playing the sample on a keyboard in time to the music. Lynott says "You're clapping your hands for me!" and again, yes they were, but that's not what we are hearing. This section is credited on the album cover as 'Cowgirl Song', although that was never a title used on any of the studio albums. Less than a minute later, the track proper comes back in for the end section.

'Dancing In The Moonlight' (from *Bad Reputation* 3:54)
Side 2 of the vinyl starts with Lynott's funky bass line, with no introductory audience noise at all. Irishman John Earle from the Graham Parker band is name-checked as the saxophonist on this version; they had been Lizzy's support act on the *Bad Reputation* tour, and his understated background playing is tastefully plaintive, over a harmony backing riff, bass and two guitars. One wonders what they would have done if they didn't have a support band with a sax player. Gorham's solo is absolutely note-perfect and fluid, but Robbo's great little wacka-wacka guitar detail just before it could easily go unnoticed. The backing vocals answer each other from opposite sides of the mix. A lovely final harmony note feeds back into the intro of the next number.

'Massacre' (from *Johnny The Fox* 2:56)
That feedback on the final note of 'Dancing In The Moonlight' makes an excellent opening salvo on this frenetic, powerful rocker and Lynott's vocals are fed into an echo box to add ominous overtones. At one point, Lynott sings "The spirit's forced to yield," but he turns away from the mic and the last two words are lost. This is one of those occasions that could easily have been fixed if he was really getting obsessive about ironing out every wrinkle, but its inclusion indicates that we are essentially hearing what was played on the night. The same could be said of the ending, where Lynott is a bit late turning the volume down on his final bass note.

'Still In Love With You' (from *Nightlife* 7:40)
He's also a bit late turning it back up for the first note of this all-time classic too! A lovely harmony guitar intro is followed by heavily chorused chords with echoey lead over the top. Really, this is tons better than the studio original in every way; the adrenalin of the last track gives way to a genuinely emotional vocal delivery. This live version is deliberately played noticeably slower than the original. Lynott drops in a line from a different song completely, where he squeezes in the words '...she had a baby by me,' from 'Brought Down,' literally the only bit of the set to be lifted from the *Shades Of A Blue Orphanage* album. Robertson's first solo is soaked in echo and he wrings every ounce of emotion from his Les Paul – it gets better as it goes through and the crowd can be heard clapping and whistling its approval at the end, and even now this solo is seen by many as the peak achievement of Robbo's contribution to the band. Robertson is dismissive and uses this as an example of why there cannot have been any major tampering with the recording after the event. In an interview with *GuitarPlayer.com* in 2012, he says:

> When we were mixing Live and Dangerous, there was one take of 'Still in Love with You' where my solo was just unbelievably brilliant. I'm not being a big head here, but when we heard that take, I went, 'That's the one.' But Phil Lynott had left his phaser on and it was turned so fast that the bass was going

'wow wow wow.' So why didn't Tony Visconti just fix the bass track? Because he couldn't overdub the bass. You know why? Because the bass stacks were next to the drums and the bass was bleeding all over the drum mikes and everything! There's your answer right there.

'Johnny the Fox Meets Jimmy The Weed' (from *Johnny The Fox* 3:43)

This version is even more aggressive than the studio version, but the groovy funk doesn't come across as well, neither does the ominous gangland vibe. Great wah solo from Robertson though. Overall it breaks up the set nicely, but there's no doubt there's a bit of a lull at this point. This version was used as the B-side for the US-only release of 'Cowboy Song'.

'Cowboy Song' (from *Jailbreak* 4:53)

Released as a US-only single with 'Johnny The Fox' on the B-side, this track opens side 3 of the original double-vinyl, and in common with side 2, it opens with no crowd noise at all. Lynott drawls the opening verse in a deep baritone, accompanied by a single guitar, a few sparse bass notes and some encouraging yells from the back of the hall – then there is an audible count from the right channel, followed by a massive harmony guitar and drum build-up. It's as tight as hell, with some lovely, subtle ride cymbal punctuation in the choruses. At three minutes, the audience is once again invited to participate and clap along. The band takes the briefest of breaths at the end before launching straight into the next song.

'The Boys Are Back In Town' (from *Jailbreak* 4:42)

Their biggest hit so far is unexpectedly placed mid-set, but the intro is absolutely inspired. At the end of 'Cowboy Song', Lynott sings 'It's the life for me...' and the band plays the final chord exactly as on the studio version – except that this time, that final chord is actually the opening chord of 'The Boys Are Back In Town'. It sounds so right and so obvious that it's hard to listen to the *Jailbreak* version now without wondering why they didn't do it then! Later on, they still used the same trick, even when 'Cowboy Song' wasn't in the set – we will get to that on the *Life* live double album. The drums drive hard, but the verses are restrained, with massive backing vocals on the chorus. This track hangs completely on the harmony guitars, which are note-perfect.

'Don't Believe a Word' (from *Johnny The Fox* 2:39)

'Thank you!' shouts Lynott, and we are straight into this adrenalin pumper. It rocks harder than any other song on the album; a genuine shame it's so short. A wonderful 'wah' solo from Robertson is a lesson in succinct wizardry. He is also turned up way loud in the verse sections, so when he hits the solo, the rhythm guitar drops out almost completely. Gorham is playing, but he's way down in the mix at this point.

'Warriors' (from *Jailbreak* 4:00)

This one is billed as 'Warrior' on the album sleeve, although it gets its original 's' back on the label. This Prog-metal piece is perfect, presenting spoken vocals with nicely-judged echo, sounding powerfully calm in front of a chugging, heavy backdrop. The superbly tight end section showcases Downey at his commanding best.

'Are You Ready' (Lynott, Gorham, Downey, Robertson, non-album 2:46)

Lynott introduces this as 'a new one'. It's a straightforward, up-tempo rock'n'roll anthem with rapid 1960s-style echo on the vocals but pretty banal lyrics. A brief harmony guitar riff at the end of each verse gives it some personality; Gorham takes the first solo with phase or chorus on it; Robertson's closing solo is uncharacteristically free of gadgetry.

'Suicide' (from *Fighting* 5:12)

Lynott starts side 4 with an understated introduction to this rumbling juggernaut of a number. The guys are driving it along, but it definitely shifts up a gear at three minutes with a breakdown leading into Gorham's first solo. There is an answering solo by Robertson, a bit of an interlude, then Gorham comes back in, with a wah pedal this time. The crash ending is much more emphatic than on the album; it certainly can't be accused of petering out this time.

'Sha La La' (from *Nightlife* 5:34)

Lynott appears to say something about 'O Solo Mio' under his breath before introducing this drum showcase, which starts with a count-in. The nicely-executed descending harmony runs are OK and Lynott does his best to deliver the vocals; Gorham plays an unusual and effects-soaked solo, but this is all about Downey's double kick-drum, which he keeps up all the way through. Most drummers of the era used a drum solo to show off every riff they know, but Downey deliberately understates his stick work here and keeps that pumping power going throughout, with a slow phaser on his drums, making them circle and soar. A minute and a half later, he slows gradually to a stop; then there is a huge crash ending with loads of echo. The eagle-eyed perfectionists amongst you may have noticed that the song title contains no hyphens on this album, unlike *Nightlife,* where is it spelt 'Sha-La-La'.

'Baby Drives Me Crazy' (Lynott, Gorham, Downey, Robertson, non-album 6:42)

Lynott seems to think the audience should know this one, although it does not appear on any studio album. They all sing along anyway. The support act on the *Johnny* tour was a Californian band named Clover, and their frontman Huey Lewis – billed as 'Bluesy Huey Lewis' on the sleeve – plays harmonica on this straightforward 12-bar mid-paced boogie. Lewis would go on to become mega in the '80s with his band The News, but he has always credited Lynott with teaching him the craft. The song is not much to write home about, being basically a vehicle for some audience interaction and for Lynott to introduce the band and throw out thanks and credits – a celebration of the gig really. Gorham is introduced as their 'candidate for the next President of the United States of America,' while he drops in a few notes of Dixie, and Robertson is introduced as 'the baby of the band,' with a special mention being made of 'his German dog.' The canine in question was Derek the Dog, a stuffed toy that Robbo bought on the road in Germany. Somehow the plush toy got to be Robbo's mascot on stage, perched atop his Marshall stack at every gig.

'The Rocker' (from *Vagabonds Of The Western World* 4:18)
The crowd is quite clearly calling for this one, and Lynott strings them along for a bit before relenting and letting Robbo loose on Eric Bell's classic intro riff. Both guitarists belt it out with relish, Downey slamming around his kit in the breaks as if it's going out of fashion. Robertson's strident solo clearly drifts from the left speaker into the middle for a few seconds towards the end before panning back out to the left again. The set finishes with a crash ending, and then we're back to the chants of 'Lizzy!... Lizzy!...', again as the audience gradually fades away.

Associated material
'Me And The Boys (Were Wondering How You And The Girls Were Getting Home From Here Tonight)' (Downey, Robertson, Lynott, Gorham 6:00)
This non-album encore number was released as the B-side to 'Rosalie', sometimes shortened to simply 'Me And The Boys' for obvious reasons. A mad, driving rocker, it starts off with thumping drums that wouldn't be amiss on an Adam And The Ants single years later, and is basically a full-on, balls to the wall rock jam, although this version is not as lunatic as some of the versions out there; the superior production separates the instruments a bit at least. It was recorded in Toronto on 28th November 1977, on the *Bad Reputation* tour, a full year after the A-side. In fact, a sound-check version of the song was included on the 2011 expanded 2-CD edition of *Bad Reputation*.

Black Rose: A Rock Legend

Released: 13 April 1979, also released in US
Label: UK Vertigo, US Mercury
Recorded at: Pathé Marconi EMI Studios, Paris, France; Good Earth Studios,
London, UK December 1978 – February 1979
Brian Downey: Drums & percussion
Scott Gorham: Lead guitar, guitars & backing vocals
Gary Moore: Lead guitar, guitars & backing vocals
Philip Lynott: Vocals, bass guitar & 12-string guitar
Huey Lewis (credited as 'Bluesy Hughie'): Harp on 'With Love' and 'Sarah'
Jimmy Bain: Bass on 'With Love'
Mark Nauseef: Drums on 'Sarah'
Produced by: Tony Visconti and Thin Lizzy
Album duration: 39 minutes
Chart position: UK: 2, US: 81

There was dismay amongst the fans when news of Robertson's departure was
announced, as it was clear that the classic chemistry would leave with him. On
the other hand, the realisation that Gary Moore would once again be joining
the fold was greeted with mouth-watering anticipation. Moore was already
known in the rock world for his awesome guitar-shredding speed, and for his
long-standing association with the Thin Lizzy name. He had been a full member
for a brief period in between *Vagabonds* and *Nightlife,* and then again during
Robertson's temporary hiatus between *Johnny The Fox* and *Bad Reputation*.
He was receptive to the Irish folk influences and Gaelic melodic phrasing
that had been evident on such classics as 'Emerald' and 'Soldier Of Fortune',
and these influences reached their natural peak with Moore in the band. He
seemed tailor-made for the part, and so it turned out; in fact, Gorham credits
Moore's arrival with rekindling his own enthusiasm and enjoyment. *Now* we
would have some fun. Moore joined in time for a tour of the US, then Australia
and Japan, playing a famous open-air gig on Sydney Harbour in front of a
massive crowd. In fact, not only had the band lost Robertson, but Downey had
also had enough – burned out and despondent, he was temporarily replaced
on these tours by American Mark Nauseef, who is generally credited with doing
an excellent job.

It wasn't all plain sailing for the album either and although Downey was
back by then, Fitzpatrick's dramatic cover art, depicting a black rose in full
bloom, flecked with drops of blood of unknown origin, turned out to be more
immediately apt than he could have known, as the band started to spiral out
of control. What cannot be denied is that Lynott was in the midst of a creative
whirlwind, not only with Lizzy but with several projects and collaborations.
He had crammed in a guest spot on *Jeff Wayne's Musical Version Of The War
Of The Worlds* playing Parson Nathaniel opposite Julie Covington as Beth;
the recording had happened in late 1976, but the album was released in June

1978. Lynott had commenced recording his first solo album with a different band of musicians. He had also settled into a stable romantic relationship with Caroline Crowther, the daughter of popular 1970s children's TV entertainer Leslie Crowther, that would progress to marriage soon afterwards. Their daughter Sarah had been born just before Christmas 1978, named for Lynott's much-loved maternal grandmother – but Phil and Scott were spiralling ever deeper into a maelstrom of harder and harder drugs, and it was in Paris during the early sessions for *Black Rose* that heroin started to take a firm hold. The sessions ended in disarray and ended up moving back to London; some tracks recorded for Lynott's solo album ended up on *Black Rose* and vice versa; often the musicians didn't even know which project they were recording for.

Many Thin Lizzy aficionados number this album amongst the best the band ever produced; but truthfully the 38 minutes is a real mix of Lizzy at their best and pretty much their worst. *Black Rose* hosts some of the most powerful, iconic numbers and soaring guitar harmonies of the band's entire catalogue, although it also includes some dross. Moore slots in like a custom-made component, and the machine runs as well as ever – some would say better – with his presence. Although Moore's scintillating guitar work was the jewel in the crown of a remarkable album, the crown itself was arguably Downey's superhuman drumming, which reached a crescendo on this set. If not every track is a winner, each one is at least backed with a tremendous avalanche of stupendous percussion.

Album cover

The front cover art, Jim Fitzpatrick's striking painting of a blood-flecked black rose (rendered in blueish purple to allow light and shade), bears the words 'Black Rose' in a complex, floral script, with the subtitle 'A Rock Legend' written beneath in small letters. On the back, the faces of the four band members are shown against the silhouette of the rose, and the title is translated into Irish Gaelic: Róisín Dubh: Finscéal Cnoc. The black rose is a long-standing metaphor for Ireland; the blood a reminder of its turbulent past, especially perhaps, its numerous wars with the English. The album is actually named after the Tudor-era Irish ballad Róisín Dubh which is said to have been to be named for the daughter of the Earl of Tyrone, and is often rendered into English as 'Dark Rosaleen'. Using English phonetics, the phrase is pronounced Ro-sheen Duv in the south and something more like Ro-sheen Doo in Northern Ireland; the word 'dubh' meaning 'black' or 'dark' can also be heard in the name of Dublin, the capital of Eire, derived from Dubhlinn meaning black pool or dark pool.

The flecks of blood on the rose are a reference to a Christian-themed poem named 'I See His Blood Upon The Rose' by Joseph Plunkett, a member of the Irish Republican Brotherhood, who was executed for his part in the Easter Rising against British rule in Ireland in 1916.

Although Thin Lizzy was Lynott's priority, he also had a number of irons in other fires at this point. Punk rock had largely pushed classic rock out of the limelight, and Lynott, concerned about going the way of the dinosaurs, had teamed Lizzy with several members of the Punk and New Wave communities to form a loose affiliation side project called the Greedy Bastards – usually paraphrased to 'The Greedies,' for obvious reasons. Black Rose's inner sleeve carried the obscure message: 'To Greedies everywhere.'

Before the album's release, Lynott reportedly ranted that the sleeves had all been printed using the wrong shade of purple, and demanded that they be withdrawn and replaced. In the event, none were withdrawn, but a smaller batch was printed with the colour corrected, Lynott was told the replacement had occurred and the release went ahead as planned, mostly using the original sleeves.

'Do Anything You Want To' (Lynott 3:53)
Released as the second single from the album on 8 June 1979, with non-album song 'Just The Two Of Us' on the B-side, the song reached no. 14 in the UK. It also made a surprise entry into the US charts, if no. 81 can be called an entry. Still, it was the first Lizzy single to touch the US charts since 'The Boys Are Back In Town'. Thrumping kettle drums and thumping bass underpin a strident dual-guitar harmony to introduce the album. The mood is upbeat and positive, with some neat feedback sustain at about two minutes. "I used to tune the tom-toms as low as I could without them starting to sound too low," Downey told the author; "I liked that deep tom sound that was going on back in the seventies and early eighties; it was just a matter of personal taste." Even so, sometimes a deep tom just isn't deep enough, and for the intro and the middle section of this song, they hired in some timpanis. He continues, "Actually if you look at the video, the whole band is using timpanis! Gary Moore, Phil, Scott and I are all playing them, but on the record, it's just me. In fact, we used to bring the timpanis on stage; we wheeled them out so all the members could play when we played it live! The guys would put their guitars round their backs, pick up the timpani sticks and start playing in the middle of the song! That was a big feature when Gary was in the band." As with 'The Boys Are Back In Town', this song highlights the harmony guitar lines, without containing any guitar solo as such. Lynott's lyrics entreat the listener to do exactly as he or she wants, without being pushed around by bullies who don't have any authority over other people's lives. For some reason, just as it is about to fade out, Lynott starts talking over the timpani outro in a faux Elvis Presley voice, lamenting the death of Elvis. This is not the same song as 'Do Anything You Wanna Do' by Eddie and the Hot Rods, which was released a couple of years earlier, just two weeks before Elvis passed away, coincidentally.

'Toughest Street In Town' (Lynott, Gorham, Moore 4:01)
Hard-rocking power chords introduce a grim urban tale of hardship and violence. We get to hear the first Moore shredding solo here, and as often happens, we wonder why he didn't use a clearer guitar tone back in the day

– impressive as it is, it's quite hard to pick out what he's playing. The backing vocals are clearly Moore and Lynott. Tough and gritty as the scene is presented in the song, with descriptions of violence and oppression, this is the toned-down version. It originally contained overt references to needle tracks on a man's arm due to shooting up heroin – or 'smack' as it is called in the song – which were rewritten on the orders of the record company. A fictional guy named Jack gets a couple of mentions in the song; Lynott must have tired of calling all his characters Johnny by this time.

'S & M' (Lynott, Downey 4:05)

Once round the drums, then fast hi-hat under wacka-wacka guitar chords introduce an unpleasant little ditty about sadomasochistic sex. Lynott was never one to shy away from controversial or contentious subjects, but there is no social message in this one other than that some people like to get the whips out. Apart from 'I Don't Want To Forget How To Jive' and possibly 'Boogie Woogie Dance', this slimy and grimy tale may just be the most pointless waste of vinyl in the Lizzy catalogue in this writer's opinion, although Gorham's solo is fast and tasteful, as well as being as clear as a bell, and the frenetic but rock-solid drumming is frankly awesome – however, the song follows a rudimentary G-Em-C-D chord progression, which is about as primitive as it gets, so it can't even really claim musical merit. As it happens, this undeserving song was one of the first numbers to be written for this album and was already being trotted out as part of the live set on the *Live And Dangerous* promotional tour, before being given another outing as the B-side to 'Do Anything You Want To' for the single's US release. Some female squealing can be heard in the background at about three minutes, just in case we didn't think the atmosphere was tacky enough. Apparently, R&B singer Rihanna recorded a song with the same title in 2010.

'Waiting For An Alibi' (Lynott 3:30)

Released as the album's lead single 23 February 1979 and peaking at no. 9 in the UK, the first single from the album in every country except the US, having 'With Love' on the B-side. In the US, 'Got To Give It Up' was the single instead, also using 'With Love' for the B-side. 'Alibi' is another early song, already written and recorded in demo form while Brian Robertson was still in the band. A short bass line introduces an ominously intense pop-rocker, leading into a classic twin-guitar intro. Although the 3½ minute album version is the same as the single, an extended version surfaced soon afterwards with a third verse and chorus missing from the original. Our protagonist, a bookmaker named Valentino, inhabits a shady world of gambling, blackmail and threat, with the third, restored verse showing his sensitive side. The production is great on this one, with plenty going on and everything clean and clear. Gorham's solo is really good, finishing on a superb series of harmony arpeggios. The extended version became *de rigeur* on Thin Lizzy compilations thereafter, and on radio plays.

'Sarah' (Lynott, Moore 3:33)

Released as a single 5 October 1979 and reaching no. 24 in the UK, the third single from the album, with 'Got To Give It Up' as an incongruous B-side, seeing as 'Sarah' is a deliriously affectionate ode to an infant daughter and 'Got To Give It Up' is a tale of descent into alcoholism and drug abuse. This was the second song in the Thin Lizzy catalogue to be named 'Sarah'; the first was named for Lynott's grandmother, who effectively raised him, and was included on *Shades Of A Blue Orphanage*. This one was written for his newborn daughter, born in December 1978 and named after her great-grandmother. It's a light and joyous ballad, with a surprisingly musical middle-eight with a melodic Moore solo and climbing background guitars. The backing is augmented by bongos, and, although uncredited, Mark Nauseef played the drums, indicating that this is one of those crossover numbers that could just as easily have ended up on Lynott's solo album. We also hear harmonica courtesy of Huey Lewis, as well as twangy harmony guitars. Gorham does not appear at all, but the story goes that Moore recorded no less than seven different guitar parts over the course of the track. Just to round things off, Judie Tzuke provided some backing vocals.

'Got To Give It Up' (Lynott 4:24)

Released as the B-side to third album single 'Sarah'. Gary Moore practices his Peter Green blues on this bravely inward-looking confessional; Lynott sings with convincing pain and pathos about his struggle with alcohol and an increasing dependence on harder and harder drugs. Some nice lulls and peaks give the song shape and colour, with a flanged Moore solo at the end. However, Lynott appears to be playing some kind of mind game with his listeners; when recording the vocals, eye-witnesses say he was standing at the mic with a glass of brandy in one hand and a spliff in the other, and snorting cocaine in between takes. The lyrics indicate that he knew exactly what it was doing to him and what he really ought to do about it, but his demeanour is defiant. For some reason, this song was released as a single in the US in preference to 'Waiting For An Alibi', which was the lead single from the album in every other country.

'Get Out Of Here' (Lynott, Midge Ure 3:37)

This basic, up-tempo pop-rocker shows Lynott acknowledging the rise of the punk culture and the apparently declining relevance of old-fashioned rock. A phased bass intro leads into a simple C-Am-F-G new wave anthem, which is the same chord structure (albeit in a different key) as 'S & M'. The vocal echo answerbacks are perfectly executed and Moore's solo is inventive and barely-restrained. It's such an un-Lizzy-like song, it's no surprise that the writer's credits include electro-pop pioneer Midge Ure from Visage with his chart-friendly pop sensibilities, but Ure himself declines to take the credit. Online music database *songfacts.com* gives another take on it:

In our interview with Ure, he explained that he and Lynott were hanging out in London when Phil came up with this song. At the time, Ure was struggling to make ends meet, and Lynott giving him a songwriter credit was a huge financial boost. 'I didn't really add an awful lot to it – he was very generous,' Ure said. 'He looked after me like a big brother.'

'With Love' (Lynott 4:38)
Released as the B-side to 'Waiting For An Alibi' in February 1979 for all countries except the US, where it was used as the B-side to 'Got To Give It Up' instead. Here is another crossover ballad, more poppy than anything else on this album. Jimmy Bain played the bass, which makes him the only bassist apart from Lynott to play on any Thin Lizzy track, and Huey Lewis stuck a bit more harmonica on it too. A glorious descending harmony guitar motif is complemented by a sweet Gary Moore solo. It's a relatively faceless track in terms of airplay and general familiarity, but it's actually a really good number, melodic and catchy, and could have been a decent single. It soars at the end with the harmony riff and improvised vocals, with more guitar soloing coming in over the top.

'Róisín Dubh (Black Rose): A Rock Legend' (7:06)
The original LP label credits the song in four parts, although this distinction is not shown on the sleeve: 'Shenendoah' (Trad), 'Will You Go Lassy Go' (F. McPeak), 'Danny Boy' (Trad) and 'The Mason's Apron' (Trad). The three traditional ones are credited as arranged by Lynott/Moore. Of course, it is much more complex than simply stringing together a load of old songs. The first minute and three quarters are entirely original, a melodic and uplifting piece with a generally Gaelic feel. First it introduces us to the legend of Cú Chulainn, whom the inner sleeve explains was 'The Hound of Ulster, the champion and the greatest of all the heroes of the Red Branch'. Cú Chulainn (or Cúchulainn) was the son of a god and a mortal woman in the Ulster Cycle of Irish mythology, and the guardian of Ulster against the evil Queen Medb (or Maeve).

There is some glorious, frenetic fast drumming in a slightly odd time signature – it alternates between bars in 3/4 and 4/4 time, so it seems to skip a beat every couple of bars – and an absolute guitarfest as the axes harmonise, then call and answer, then harmonise again. Lynott started to develop the piece during Robertson's tenure, and the idea was to include traditional songs from wide-ranging sources – but it was voted just a bit corny and even though the concept was reportedly in full rehearsal while Robbo was still around, it never fully materialised until Moore joined the band and got behind the idea. The lyrics branch off into a reference to 'The Mountains Of Mourne,' a song by Irishman Percy French at the close of the nineteenth century. At 1:45 we are treated to an abrupt change, as the guitar starts to pick out the tune to 'Shenendoah', which is actually a traditional American song, but fits the mood of the piece perfectly. Lynott extemporises the vocals to some extent, and it morphs imperceptibly into the Scottish-Irish ballad 'Wild Mountain Thyme' (otherwise known as 'Will Ye Go Lassie Go'); thus a nod is given to both Gorham's and Robertson's homelands. At 2:10 we hear a few bars of an instrumental rendition of the traditional Irish 'Danny Boy' (or 'Londonderry Air' – it's the same tune). From 2:33 the guys riff on these and similar chord progressions, changing again from 3:18 to a traditional-style Irish jig or reel. The tune is rolling like a river, washing joyously over the listener until 4:04 when everything stops and Moore goes into his showpiece – a manically fast interpretation of 'The Mason's Apron', a reel with Moore playing both the calling and answering guitars.

Everything stops at the five-minute mark and Lynott sings a slow section with a mandolin-style guitar and synthy keyboard-washed backing, then everything goes into the outro – Lynott puts in as many Irish-related references as he can: Róisín Dubh, novelist James Joyce, poet William Butler Yeats, playwright Oscar Wilde, writer Brendan Behan, 1964 movie *Girl With Green Eyes* (adapted by Irish novelist Edna O'Brien from her book *The Lonely Girl*), Dark Rosaleen, (another incarnation of Róisín Dubh), footballer George Best, singer Van Morrison, a glancing reference to the Irish potato famine of the 19th century, Thin Lizzy's own traditional hit 'Whisky In The Jar', John Synge's play *The Playboy Of The Western World,* The Mountains of Mourne in Northern Ireland and music hall singalong 'It's A Long Way To Tipperary'. He's still adding to the list as the song eventually fades out, over seven minutes after it started.

Associated Material
'Just The Two Of Us' (Lynott, Gorham 2:47)
This non-album song saw the light of day as the B-side to 'Do Anything You Want To'. It's an up-tempo, pleasantly melodic pop song, with a decent structure and a fair bit of soul, which from this writer's perspective would have been a decent addition to the album, especially if it meant ditching 'S & M' in the process. As it happens though, 'S & M' was used instead of this worthy number as the B-side for the US release of the aforementioned single.

'Parisienne Walkways' (Lynott, Moore 3:08)
Released as a single in April 1979 and climbing to no. 8 in the UK charts, this is not a Thin Lizzy song at all, but a Gary Moore solo track from his 1978 album *Back On The Streets*. However, with Moore's utterly sublime guitar melody making it a massive UK hit, and Lynott's distinctive voice guesting as lead vocalist, it has become so far associated with Lynott and Lizzy that it regularly appears on greatest hits packages, which are sometimes billed as 'Phil Lynott and Thin Lizzy' compilations in order to find an excuse to stick it on. Many perhaps don't realise that Downey also played the drums on this song, making it the same trio that recorded Lizzy's last single for Decca, 'Little Darling'.

Lynott and Downey also played on two other songs on the album, 'Fanatical Fascists', a fast, punky anthem also written by Lynott, and Moore's down-tempo ballad version of 'Don't Believe A Word'. These two songs featured Moore on vocals though, and are therefore not so recognisably Thin Lizzy-related. In an article by Richard Buskin for *SoundOnSound.com* in 2012, Engineer Chris Tsangarides claims that the song was originally written as an instrumental, which makes perfect sense, seeing as the guitar melody screams on underneath the vocal sections, and Moore tended to miss out the second verse vocals completely when playing it live, just concentrating on the guitar line. The title was already there, so Lynott apparently made up the lyrics to fit. Buskin also claims that the opening line on the original sheet music said, 'I remember Paris in the fall tonight,' although this was changed before recording took place; the line as recorded on the actual song contains an autobiographical pun: 'I remember Paris in '49.' This could easily be a reference to Lynott's father, Cecil Parris, in Lynott's birth year, 1949. A couple of interesting recording snippets: Lynott played those three descending intro notes on an electric upright bass rather than a bass guitar. And for the long, sustained guitar note that introduced the main solo, an effect which is notoriously difficult to achieve on demand, Moore reportedly left a big gap and played the rest of the song around it. Then he went back and dubbed in the long note afterwards. This is borne out by live recordings of the song, in which it sometimes takes Moore two or three attempts to get that note started.

During the same sessions, Moore also recorded a song named 'Spanish Guitar' with a very similar chord structure, and with vocals by Lynott. Moore released it as a non-album single with his own vocals, so it doesn't make it into this list on its own merits; nevertheless, the version with Lynott's vocals was (apparently accidentally) released in Sweden through official channels and is also available on various bootleg compilations such as the massive seven-CD *Phil Lynott: The Man And His Music*.

'A Night In The Life Of A Blues Singer' (Lynott 5:44)

This non-album recording from the *Black Rose* sessions was used as one of the B-sides on the 12" single of 'Nineteen', Lynott's last-ever single, and also appeared on the massive 4-CD retrospective *Warriors Kings Vagabonds Angels* in 2001. Eventually, of course, it also turned up on the 2011 expanded 2-CD edition of *Black Rose*. A descending, bluesy backing riff and slow shuffle rhythm make for a late-night, downbeat lament with something of the flavour of the old Decca days. It builds up to a screaming solo from Moore, but the whole thing was probably just a bit too far from the frenetic beat of most of the album to make the final cut.

'Rockula' (or 'Rock Your Love') (Jimmy Bain 4:16)

This non-album demo was included on the 2011 2-CD edition of *Black Rose*. Recorded at Ramport Studios in Battersea in January 1978, a year before most of the *Black Rose* recordings took place, it features the same line-up in a pretty loose, rough and ready minor-key pop-rocker. Incidentally, a mock-horror rock movie with this name, featuring disparate pop and rock stars, appeared in 1990. The plot involves a band named 'Rockula', whose frontman is a vampire. It didn't have anything to do with Thin Lizzy but does at least give a clue to the meaning of the song's name. The title is a pun on 'Dracula', with the lyrics accusing the character Rockula of being bent on destruction. However, without an official album release, it's down to the listener to decide what Lynott is actually singing, and it sounds enough like 'Rock Your Love' for this to be listed as the song title in many cases – although various spellings crop up on various sources.

'Cold Black Night' (Moore 3:37)
This non-album demo was another one included on the 2011 2-CD edition of *Black Rose*. It's a straight 12-bar in the 1970s pub-rock vein, and could easily have been recorded by The Bluesbreakers or any number of blues bands – in fact, it is quite reminiscent of 'Loved Another Woman' by Peter Green's Fleetwood Mac. The version presented on the deluxe *Black Rose* was recorded in The Bahamas and includes harmonica backing, but there is also a demo recorded at Ramport Studios in January 1978, which has a more primitive Dr Feelgood-like pub rock feel.

'Hate' (Lynott 3:18)
This punky demo was recorded at Ramport Studios, Battersea, in February 1978 by the *Black Rose* line-up. It's an anthem against hate with a staccato backing, reminiscent of 'Fighting My Way Back', at least at the start. Lynott had another go at it in 1982 with his second solo album, but it still didn't make the final cut.

'Song For Jimi' (4:50)
In 1980, Lynott reunited with Eric Bell to record this tribute to Jimi Hendrix on the tenth anniversary of his death. It's a psychedelic rocker, with manically frenetic drumming and laconic, heavy-lidded vocals in the Hendrix style. Originally released only on a flexi-disc featuring four bands given away with *Flexipop* magazine, it didn't see an album release until the 4-CD retrospective *Vagabonds Kings Warriors Angels* in 2001. By then though, Bell's lead guitar track had apparently been lost and that version features no solo at all. The original flexi-disc version was resurrected on the 1994 bootleg mega-compilation *Phil Lynott: The Man And His Music*. Although Downey is officially credited as the drummer, thus reuniting the original Thin Lizzy line-up, there is a short cowbell section in the middle that some say was added by Mark Nauseef, and there is a strong assertion among a sizeable number of fans that Nauseef drummed the whole track.

'A Merry Jingle' (Lynott, Downey, Gorham, Paul Cook, Steve Jones 3:09)
Released in December 1979 as a Christmas single in the UK and reaching no. 28, this song and its B-side 'A Merry Jangle' (which was simply 'A Merry Jingle'

played backwards), were the only official recordings to be offered by the Thin Lizzy/Sex Pistols mash-up known as the Greedies. The various celebrities, Bob Geldof, Jimmy Bain, Chris Spedding, Gary Moore et al., were slimmed down to just Lynott, Gorham and Downey, plus Paul Cook and Steve Jones from the Pistols. They might have had fun making it, but despite airing on *Top Of The Pops,* it more or less sank without trace. It makes it to this list though, by virtue of sneaking on to a year-2000 2-CD Thin Lizzy limited edition Swedish compilation named *The Boys Are Back In Town*.

Chinatown

Released: UK 10 October 1980, US 29 October 1980
Label: UK Vertigo, US Warner Bros.
Recorded at: Good Earth Studios, London, UK, April – August 1980
Brian Downey: Drums
Philip Lynott: Bass guitar, keyboards, vocals
Scott Gorham: Lead guitar & guitars, backing vocals
Snowy White: Lead guitar & guitars
Darren Wharton: Keyboards & backing vocals
Midge Ure: Backing vocals on 'Chinatown'
Fiachra Trench: String arrangement on 'Didn't I'
Tim Hinkley: Electric piano on 'Didn't I' (spelt Hinckley on the album)
Produced by: Thin Lizzy and Kit Woolven
Album duration: 41 minutes
Chart position: UK: 7, US: 120

Chinatown polarises opinion like no other album in the Lizzy catalogue. The out-and-out rockers amongst their fanbase see this set as a triumph, whereas fans of Lynott's more sensitive and creative side hold it at arm's length. In fact, opinion remains polarised about all of the band's output from this point onwards. Given his track record, Gary Moore was always likely to be a stop-gap measure, but frustrated by Lizzy's shambolic descent into anarchy, he ended up walking out on the band in the middle of their US tour in support of *Black Rose*. At least the band was not left as a duo as it was when Eric Bell blew up mid-gig, but ironically, twin guitars were now so ingrained within Lizzy's sound that it was not possible to continue with just one guitarist. A hasty call was made to Midge Ure, who flew out to join the tour, hurriedly trying to learn the songs while in the air. Ure recounted the circumstances in an interview with Paul Whimpenny for *Rock Society* magazine in 2019:

I was putting Visage together and finishing the first album and I got a phone call in the studio one night. It was Phil Lynott saying, 'I'm in Arkansas in the middle of nowhere and Gary Moore is out of the band, and we're opening as special guests for Journey and playing these mega domes. Can you come over tomorrow and finish the tour because we've got three weeks to go yet?' I went home that night and they'd left me a bunch of cassettes, a setlist, a plane ticket, a tour itinerary, and a message, 'Can I come to pick you up at 6 o'clock in the morning?' I packed my bags. I got my ghetto blaster because I wanted to listen to the cassettes on the plane and learn the set. And when I got to the airport, I saw that they'd put me on Concorde. It only took three hours to get to New York so I'd only actually learnt two songs by the time we landed! I then spent my first 24 hours in America – I'd never been there before – in a hotel room in New Orleans learning all the harmony guitar parts for all the Thin Lizzy songs and then the next night I was on stage doing it. It was great!

As an exponent of electro-glam pop, Ure wouldn't have been an obvious choice to many, but his musical CV is wide and varied and he certainly helped the band out of a jam. For the Japanese leg of the tour, Dave Flett from Manfred Mann's Earth Band was recruited on guitar, and Ure switched to playing keyboards, the first time the touring band had included a keyboard player since the Bob Wrixon days. Meanwhile, Lynott went shopping for a new permanent guitarist and settled on Snowy White, Dave Gilmour's wingman in the touring incarnation of Pink Floyd. He also acknowledged the rising New Wave Of Heavy Metal by hiring a keyboard player to update the sound in the shape of teenaged Darren Wharton, a musical prodigy with whizzy fingers, a mature style and the potential to add an extra layer to the cake. Jim Fitzpatrick was firmly back in the fold as well and stumped up a strikingly colourful Chinese dragon to adorn the front cover.

Snowy White was not an intuitive choice for many Lizzy fans; the band had set out a completely new stall with the hard-rocking *Live and Dangerous,* which had been presaged by *Bad Reputation's* imaginative riffage and reinforced by *Black Rose's* unabashed guitar shredding. Lizzy were now a heavy rock band, but Snowy was not a heavy rock guitarist. Pink Floyd are the master purveyors of subtle atmosphere, and Lynott likely chose White for exactly that reason. Indeed, Snowy had such a gift for feel that he had deputised for the master of the delicate touch, Peter Green, during a period when the mentally messed-up Green was not really in any state to play on his own solo albums.

So Lynott had written a set of hard-rocking songs but seemed to have chosen a mismatched musician to play them. Furthermore, although Darren Wharton could have fitted into almost any hard rock band, Lizzy were unashamedly a guitar band. They had never had a full-time keyboard player and arguably didn't need one; he was hired as a session player at this point, but it's difficult to pick out any place on the album where his contribution made any material difference to the track.

Worst of all though, Tony Visconti had refused any more involvement with the rapidly deteriorating, undisciplined rabble that Thin Lizzy were becoming, so production duties had fallen to his team, and it didn't really work. It's clear that Kit Woolven was moving the sound into the '80s, which means the heavy guitar riffs are given a twangy and lightweight treatment, the lyrics and guitar solos are quiet, the drums are given a lighter quality and the whole ambience is thickly foggy. And just to put the icing on the cake, Lynott the poet had gone AWOL and the whole album barely produced one decent lyric.

Album cover

The Good Earth Studios are situated in Soho in London, a district adjacent to – and virtually synonymous with in most people's minds – Chinatown, named for its strong oriental influence and populace. Fitzpatrick is back in the frame once more and outdoes himself with a stunningly colourful, eye-catching and obsessively detailed image of a Chinese dragon with laser spotlights glaring from its eyes. The band name and album name are picked out in two-inch high letters in a mock oriental script; the back cover (there is no gatefold), presents a front view of the dragon's intimidating head (or a dragon at least, this one has a lot more teeth), with the laser eyes and bloodied fangs. The inner sleeve carries a short paragraph explaining the phenomenon of Chinatown, which is a concept not limited to London where this album was recorded, but in many large Western cities. It also explains that when the dragon was used as the insignia of the Chinese Emperors, it is always depicted with five claws on each foot, but the three-clawed dragon on the cover is the mark of the Triads, the massively powerful organised crime syndicates based in China – these organisations had been a bit of an obsession with Lynott since the *Bad Reputation* days, as indicated by the lyrical content of the song 'Opium Trail' on that album.

'We Will Be Strong' (Lynott 5:07)

The album starts promisingly enough, in the tradition set by *Black Rose*, with a powerful harmony guitar intro to a melodic rock song in Lizzy's trademark quick chord-change format. Snowy White proves himself an able axeman and his harmonies match Gorham with split-second perfection. The song itself is a mid-tempo, fairly unobtrusive blue-collar anthem to the power of the working man. The solo comes through loud and clear, but then the atmosphere dips alarmingly when the verse comes back in. It's a decent song, but not really strong enough to carry the five minutes plus allotted to it. Another guitar solo rides easily underneath the repeated vocals towards the end; then a harmony guitar passage leads to a final power chord. Released as a US-only single with 'Sweetheart' on the B-side.

'Chinatown' (Downey, Gorham, Lynott, White 4:40)

The lead single from the album, released on 16 May 1980, with a live version of 'Sugar Blues' on the B-side, in which Lynott is introducing the newcomer Snowy White. Nearly making the top 20, it stalled at no. 21 on the UK chart. This song was not released in the States though; it may have been considered a somewhat UK-centric theme, although there are Chinatown districts in the US, including several in New York City alone. The song is a sincere attempt to recapture the glory days, with a complex, hard-driving intro and a chugging rhythm. A classic rock riff à la Free or the original Fleetwood Mac morphs through further riffs and a drum roll into a driving rock number in the vein of 'Don't Believe A Word', although the lyrics are a pretty banal attempt to conjure up the degradation and depravity of London's red-light district. An evil laugh at two minutes presages a restrained section with a strident solo, and an extra couple of beats cleverly laid in every four bars, giving a frisson of musical interest. The second solo is accompanied by a change in chord progression and a bit of an uplift in mood; a well-constructed chord sequence and a final harmony riff lead nicely to a tight ending. For the first time, we find that the

83

vocals are actually too high in the mix – it's a great, rocking song but could have been a metal classic if more emphasis was placed on the bludgeoning riff and less on the lyrics, which simply aren't strong enough to take precedence. Midge Ure is credited with backing vocals.

'Sweetheart' (Lynott 3:28)
A heavy start gives way to an up-tempo, melodic pop-rocker. There are some tight harmony vocals in the chorus, but Lynott's voice is taking on a distinctly nasal quality here. Again, it's a catchy and passable enough melody to make a decent B-side, but it simply isn't strong enough to be anything but filler on a full-length LP. Fittingly, it made the B-side on the US-only release of 'We Will Be Strong'.

'Sugar Blues' (Downey, Gorham, Lynott, White 4:18)
A fast rocker that benefits from the use of headphones: don a pair of bins and you can hear that the utterly simplistic but heavily rhythmic, chugging guitar backing seems to rock left and right in the pan with the two guitars playing it, which is a pretty neat effect. It's a totally unabashed homage to the junkie life though; Lynott seems to have given up any scheme to 'give it up', claiming that the 'sugar' of the title adds 'a little sweetness' to his life, while also admitting that it is causing him to worry about his health. The 1980s-style blandness rules the production, unfortunately; the drum rolls are performed on hollow-sounding biscuit tin toms, but there are some excellent fast, short harmony guitar phrases and a driving solo. Lynott chose this track to introduce Snowy White on his first round of touring, which includes a dark pun, intentionally or otherwise: Sugar is, of course, a euphemism for cocaine, but then so is Charlie Snow or just snow. Lynott's introduction to White's solo on the live version of the track that adorns the B-side of the 'Chinatown' single is therefore apt: 'We've got someone to add a little sweetness to your life – Snowy White on lead guitar.'

'Killer On The Loose' (Lynott 3:53)
Released as the second single on 9 September 1980 and climbing to a creditable no. 10 in the UK, with the non-album song 'Don't Play Around' on the B-side, except in the US where 'Sugar Blues' adorned the back and it failed to chart. Never one to shy away from dark subject matter, nevertheless Lynott arguably sails far too close to the wind with this one. A serial killer was at large in Yorkshire in northern England at the time, with a penchant for the brutal murder of mostly (but not exclusively) prostitutes, and a tendency to flaunt his crimes under the nose of a hard-pressed police force. Inevitably, his doings brought to mind the notorious Victorian villain Jack the Ripper, and the unknown assailant was dubbed the Yorkshire Ripper by the press. While all this was front-page news, and well before the Ripper was brought to justice, Lizzy released this hard-driving shouty rocker as a single. Continuing where

'S & M' left off, some of the vocals breach the bounds of good taste or even acceptability. Lynott was taken to task in the press about it at the time, and protested that the song was a warning, not a glorification of violence. The deep baritone spoken section is gradually slowed down and dips deeper and deeper to another evil laugh.

One of the hardest, most potentially powerful backing riffs Lizzy ever produced drives a juggernaut rocking song, and it's a good number from that perspective without doubt, certainly a musical highlight of the album, but lyrically in the worst possible taste. To compound the sin, Lizzy used this as an audience participation number in their live shows, with the crowd joyfully belting out, "There's a killer on the loose again! A lady killer on the loose!" Back in the real world, an ordinary and unremarkable Yorkshireman named Peter Sutcliffe was eventually arrested for the Ripper crimes and proved to have committed at least 13 murders over more than a decade in addition to several other attempts. More evil slowed-down laughs at the end drive home the humour. The 'Killer On The Loose'/'Don't Play Around' 7" single was also issued as a special 2-disc gatefold single with a 7" live bonus disc of 'Chinatown' (recorded at the Hammersmith Odeon, London, 29 May 1980) and 'Got To Give It Up' (recorded at Royal Dublin Society Hall, Dublin, 7 June 1980). The song also did duty as the B-side for the Germany-only release of 'Hey You'.

'Having A Good Time' (White, Lynott 4:35)
A jolly ode to drunkenness and out-of-control partying. It's an up-tempo, good-time piece of work, with the guitarists being name-checked for the solos in turn, but really this is unabashed filler. Lynott launches into a largely improvised bit of chat at the end, 'speaking from the top of his head' as he says.

'Genocide (The Killing Of The Buffalo)' (Lynott 5:05)
Lynott returns to the western theme again; this is an anthem to the North American bison and the Native Americans, with imaginative use of toms from Downey. Lynott puts on his socially-aware hat for this one, and it's a song with a message about oppression, racism, and the careless destruction of nature. Several false endings present themselves, and the piece could probably have done with any one of them being the actual ending because once again, it's not really strong enough for the full five minutes allotted to it. Strangely for Thin Lizzy, this song features neither harmony guitar work nor any guitar solo, not that these are compulsory, but it probably would have given it a little more shape and colour. It's all said and done by the four-minute mark, but then we loop back into a full minute's repetition of the words 'The killing of the buffalo-oo, which sounds like it should have been a fade-out, but instead Downey taps once around the toms and the song fizzles to a halt.

'Didn't I' (Lynott 4:25)

The two final songs have something of the burned-out flavour of filler about them, but in fact, they are both good songs and the performances are excellent. This is one of those slow, regretful, late-night smoky ballads with string machine backing and melodic guitar interludes with some more nice tom work. After a minute, it drifts into a more coherent, sad song with synthy chords. A nice ascending harmony guitar riff leads into a majestic, major-key power chord ending.

'Hey You' (Downey, Lynott 5:06)

A funky but slightly tinny bass intro is accompanied by echo-heavy highly-strung guitar chords. After two and a half minutes, another downbeat lament about homelessness, street crime and inequality morphs into a hard rocker with a fast solo, then a false ending leads back into the intro section, with piano chords subtly in the background. It rises a bit towards the end, with up-tempo drums, shouty vocals and background lead guitar under the backing vocals before fading out. Musically, it is a superbly-executed piece, but it's hardly joyous. The song made it to a Germany-only single release in January 1981, with 'Killer On The Loose' on the B-side.

Associated material
'Don't Play Around' (Gorham, Lynott 4:22)

This hard-driving pop-rocker was the B-side to the single release of 'Killer On The Loose' in the UK, Europe and Australia, with 'Sugar Blues' being selected instead for the US release. A hard-hitting, minor key melodic metal charger in the New Wave vein, it would be more than worthy enough to make the cut in the company of the other tracks on this album, but perhaps even Phil Lynott's sensibilities drew back from this one. Another story of violence against women, the singer seems to concur with the lethal judgment meted out against the object of the song for the crime of 'playing around'. She dies in a pool of blood to the accompaniment of power chords and a fast, driving rhythm. It's debatable whether the A or B-side would draw more ire from the politically correct brigade, but this writer is staying well out of it.

Solo in Soho

Phil Lynott's debut solo album was released on 18 April 1980, a year after *Black Rose* and six months ahead of *Chinatown*. It is not strictly a Thin Lizzy album of course, but worth a mention here because of the strong presence of the band members in various combinations. Recorded at the same studios at the same time, it was perhaps inevitable that tracks originally intended for one ended up on the other and vice versa. For instance, Lynott and Downey are joined on tribute to Elvis 'King's Call' (Lynott 3:37), by guitarist Mark Knopfler of Dire Straits, whose third album *Making Movies* was released a week after *Chinatown*. Knopfler's utterly distinctive guitar style and Lynott's equally distinctive drawl make this a true hybrid of the two bands. Electro-pop piece 'Yellow Pearl', co-written by Midge Ure, had the distinction (in remixed form) of displacing the version of Led Zeppelin's 'Whole Lotta Love' as the theme tune of BBC's *Top Of The Pops* for five years; the remix was included on Lynott's second solo album the following year. Almost every track benefits from the attentions of at least one member of Thin Lizzy in addition to Lynott. Having said that, the only tracks that will merit special attention in this publication are those which were released at some time or other under the Thin Lizzy banner, starting with the album's lead single below.

'Dear Miss Lonely Hearts' (Lynott, Jimmy Bain 4:09)

This track was the lead single from Phil Lynott's debut solo album *Solo In Soho*, but is elevated to full Thin Lizzy status by the inclusion of a live version of the track on Lizzy's *Killers Live* EP, discussed below. Co-written by Rainbow bassist Jimmy Bain, this laid-back croon is a 1960s pastiche, using a chord pattern lifted straight from 'Runaround Sue', 'Under The Moon Of Love', or any one of a hundred teeny-bopper '60s hits. The lyric is based on the Agony Aunt concept, one of those newspaper columns where people write in baring their heart and soul and begging for help from some kindly mumsy type. In this case, our hero has started dating a girl, while foolishly falling in love with her sister, and doesn't know what to do, so writes a letter to Miss Lonely Hearts, crooned in relaxed style by Lynott. Spoiler alert: It doesn't end happily. The song is performed by Lynott, Downey, Gorham and White – the full set in other words.

Killers Live EP

Released 16 April 1981 during Snowy White's tenure, although not all songs feature Snowy, this EP reached no. 19 in the UK. Next to Live And Dangerous, this is probably the band's most eagerly sought-after live work, as it includes one or two (depending on the format), massive tracks that were left off that album. Released in 7" format (nevertheless to be played at 33rpm), with three songs, 12" format with four, and also in a Canadian limited edition with six, there is plenty here for the completist collector. Most importantly, all versions include 'Bad Reputation' recorded at the Tower Theatre in Philadelphia on 20 October 1977, making it the same series of gigs that provided some of the material for *Live And Dangerous*. The other two songs that appear on all versions are the familiar 'Are You Ready', and 'Dear Miss Lonely Hearts', a Phil Lynott solo piece that nevertheless made it into Thin Lizzy's live set during the Snowy White era, and is here listed as a Thin Lizzy track. These two songs were recorded at RDS Hall in Dublin on 7 June 1980, the same gig that provided the live version of 'Got To Give It Up' that was included on the bonus disc of the gatefold 7" release of 'Killer On The Loose'.

The 12" version also includes 'Opium Trail' recorded at the same gig as this version of 'Bad Reputation' – we, therefore, have Gorham and Robertson at their peak playing two of the best songs from *Bad Reputation,* their current album at the time. The quality is there, both songs rock like hell and it's difficult to think of any reason why they would not have been included on *Live And Dangerous* in the first place – except perhaps for the obvious question, 'What would you leave off?' 'Bad Reputation' includes a drum solo, which would have meant leaving off 'Sha La La', as not even the most self-indulgent of live albums includes *two* drum solos. It's only a personal opinion, but I would have gone with 'Bad Reputation' without a moment's hesitation. Incidentally, the sleeve notes erroneously state that these tracks were recorded at the Seneca College Fieldhouse, Toronto, Canada, which was another series of source gigs for *Live And Dangerous.*

The two extra songs included on the six-track Canadian version of the EP were a live version of 'Chinatown' recorded at the Hammersmith Odeon on 29 May 1980, the same gig that provided the material for the live bonus EP packaged with *Thunder And Lightning,* and 'Got To Give It Up' from the RDS Hall gig mentioned above.

Renegade

Released: UK 20 November 1981, US 27 January 1982
Label: UK Vertigo, US Warner Bros
Recorded at: Compass Point Studio, Nassau, The Bahamas, and Odyssey Studio
and Morgan Studio, London, UK, January-September 1981
The band are credited by name and by photo, but not by instrument:
Philip Lynott (Bass guitar, vocals)
Scott Gorham (Guitars, backing vocals)
Brian Downey (Drums, percussion)
Snowy White (Guitars, backing vocals)
Darren Wharton (uncredited) Keyboards, organ, Minimoog, backing vocals
Produced by: Thin Lizzy and Chris Tsangarides
Album duration: 41 minutes
Chart position: UK: 38, US: 157

Snowy White's contribution to *Chinatown* had been accepted with polite
approbation, but he hadn't exactly set the audience alight. Darren Wharton
on keyboards, who had been initially hired as a temp, was now promoted to
full membership, but no one really knew why Thin Lizzy suddenly needed
a keyboard player. What's more, the album seemed to have stepped back
from the harder-rocking direction of the past few, into more measured,
contemplative territory. Lynott was now working on his second solo album
at the same time, and Producer Kit Woolven was tearing his hair out, as he
had a different sound in mind for each of the two albums, and it was virtually
impossible to decipher which album he was engineering at any given recording
session. The scene was set for a chaotic disaster. In the end, Woolven was
delegated to produce the solo album and Chris Tsangarides was drafted in to
produce *Renegade*.

But the thing is, it all worked. In contrast with the last album, the production
on this one is pin-sharp and tight, with plenty going on, and whole tracks are
written around Wharton's keyboards, which are given room to breathe and a
spotlight to shine. And finally, we can see why Snowy White was selected, as
his tasteful twanging suits some of these songs to a tee. Brian Downey said, in
conversation with the author:

Snowy was a great guitar player; I don't know why all the criticism came up. It
was just because the image was weird; he wasn't your regular guitar gunslinger
kind of guy. He was laid back, he didn't move too much like all the other guys
did, but what he played was just superb! And I liked him as a guy; I got on
quite well with Snowy, and he got on well with everybody else – maybe apart
from Phil!

To add extra savour to the set, hard drugs notwithstanding, Lynott the poet
is back, at least in fits and starts. Thin Lizzy's increasingly hard-rocking fan

base was left scratching its collective head as a new, softer Thin Lizzy made an appearance, and many of them consigned this one to the scrapheap without a second listen. But they were simply wrong...

Album Cover

The story goes that the album was still unnamed, basically just a disparate pile of songs destined to end up on one or other of the next Thin Lizzy album or the next solo Phil Lynott album. A preoccupied Lynott was tramping the streets in frustration, (or on the tour bus, depending on which variant of the story you read), when a motorcyclist rode past, sporting both a Thin Lizzy patch on his jacket and another patch bearing the word 'Renegade'. A light bulb briefly flared above Lynott's head, as the album gained not only a name and a theme, but inspiration for its title track.

Jim Fitzpatrick had some extended talks with Lynott about artwork for the album, but the label ended up going with a photograph by Graham Hughes of a red flag, bearing a single gold star, mounted on a medieval halberd held aloft by a man's arm; the man himself is not visible.

Each of the four regular band members gets to pose holding the flag for a named photo on the back cover, but neither on the outer or inner sleeve are there any band credits, so Wharton doesn't even get a mention except as co-writer on some of the songs. The red and gold colour scheme makes for an attractive if somewhat understated cover; the sparsest of album credits on the inner sleeve are printed in gold on a red background and are therefore almost unreadable. In line with the Lizzy tradition of supplying a short story or informative paragraph though, a passage from the title track is printed on the inner sleeve.

Fitzpatrick did create an insert poster for the album, which is a very rare find if one turns up nowadays. It consisted of four band member portraits (again, no Wharton), arranged in a square formation with the words 'Thin Lizzy' in relatively small print at the top. On his own website *jimfitzpatrick.com*, he says:

> When the new album Renegade was released I was disappointed that my own ideas went unused – I had drawn up a few cool ideas too – and I still have no idea why but I would guess with the declining fortunes of the band due to Philip's excessive spending allied to his obvious drug use combined to put off any spending on artwork. ... Anyway, what did bother me as a perfectionist was the rubbish reproduction of the final poster insert. It was shite.

'Angel Of Death' (Lynott, Wharton 6:18)

Never mind the adrenaline-soaked opening power chord of *Jailbreak* and *Live And Dangerous;* this set opens unobtrusively with a single, sub-deep note, leading to an understated, gradually building atmospheric synth solo. You'll really have to have your ears on to hear it, but right at the beginning, Lynott's voice is heard deep down in the mix, crying, 'Oh my God – there's millions of them!' Downey introduces a rapid rhythm on the hi-hat, with a rumbling bass following soon afterwards. The power chords, when they appear, simply add to a sophisticated backing rather than taking the song to a different level. Eventually, Lynott's vocals come in, heralding doom and destruction. It's actually a symphonic prog rock masterpiece, with Phil playing someone like the mad priest from *War Of the Worlds,* portending the fulfilment of Nostradamus' apocalyptic prophecies. The guitar solo at three minutes is clear and fast, while still tasteful. Towards four minutes, the power subsides and Wharton starts into another smooth, legato keyboard section, with two slightly different versions following each other from each side of the mix. These may even be two takes of same the solo, as they imitate each other in theme and structure, although not note for note until they both settle into the same repeating riff where Phil's spoken voice comes in over the top – again, two voices in juxtaposition. One of the voices is slowed down, or at least heavily effected, so an ominous growl is paired with Lynott's usual speaking voice. To put the listener's mind at rest, may we just add that Lynott's father didn't die in screaming pain from an unknown disease with a helpless Phil at his bedside; that verse of the song at least is fictional. A few shards of keyboard detritus drop to the ground at the end, and again, right down in the mix, a few words are spoken – something like: 'I think they're – gone now…'

'Renegade' (Lynott, White 6:08)

Suddenly, after an extended absence, the poet in Lynott resurfaces. And a great poem too, an ode to a loner, a misfit, a bad boy to be sure, but with some of the romance of the great outlaws – a modern-day Rob Roy, a Ned Kelly, a wandering loner. The musical timing is odd, particularly in the intro; a couple of beats are skipped every few bars, but the guitar arpeggios carry on uninterrupted, so it's difficult to work out the timing. Lynott was an outspoken critic of the prog oeuvre with its self-conscious complexity, but at least here we see another example of Lizzy's ability to diverge from the rock standard without flinching. An extract from the lyrics is reproduced on the inner sleeve. In an interview with Tony Bacon for *Reverb.com,* Phil said:

> There's the description of the renegade at the start, and then I go on with why it's important that there are some people that are rebellious. Because they can start an idea, and through that some good can be achieved.

Describing the narrative of the song, he continued:

> I started it with the verses being slow, building up to the power of the chorus. That's showing the power of the renegade. And then it goes through a turmoil section … that's where we go into that sort of bizarre tempo. Then after the turmoil, there's the calm, the resolve.

A cut-down 5:25 version was also included as a bonus track on the 2013 expanded CD release.

'The Pressure Will Blow' (Lynott, Gorham 3:46)
The first 'traditional' Lizzy track on the album, with harmony guitars in the intro. Deep, sub-woofer synth notes intrude at intervals. As with many a Thin Lizzy track, the ending appears suddenly and unexpectedly, but it's crisp and tight at least. The subject of the song is, evidently, frustration, but the object of the frustration is not clear.

'Leave This Town' (Gorham, Lynott 3:49)
Lynott admitted that this one was influenced by Texan hard rockers ZZ Top, although that band would not break into the mainstream in Britain until their 1983 album *Eliminator*. They had been going for some while as a bluesy, hard-driving power trio though, with an emphasis on no-nonsense, down-home, charging rock'n'roll. 'Leave This Town' certainly shares a sensibility with some of their output, notably their 1975 single 'Tush'. This song features some nice harmony vocals, and a passage is spoken in a slow drawl, involving the Sheriff, his daughter and various lethal firearms, explaining in some detail why the protagonist feels it necessary to leave this town.

'Hollywood (Down On Your Luck)' (Gorham, Lynott 4:09)
The only single to be released in the UK from the album, in cut-down 3:18 form, this one benefitted from several B-sides: 'The Pressure Will Blow' was the main contender, with Mexican Blood' being used in the Netherlands and non-album song 'Girls' in Canada. An extended 6:16 version was also included as a bonus track on the 2013 expanded CD release. It's a pretty conventional rock song about being down on your luck in a rich town, but it was also, unfortunately, the clearest barometer to date of Thin Lizzy's falling fortunes. Lizzy had released a single named 'Trouble Boys' ahead of the release of the album (see the 'Associated material' section below), which crept into the fringes of the charts but died the death so badly, it was hurriedly withdrawn from the finished album before it hit the streets. Sadly, however, 'Hollywood' peaked at exactly the same chart position at no. 53. It was released three months after the album, and the label refused to put out a promo video for it, which was pretty unforgivable in the '80s and tantamount to not promoting it at all. They did stump up for a picture disc though, in the UK at least. This song has the distinction of being played on British TV show *Jim'll Fix It,* with a granny in her 70s playing keyboards and doing backing vocals. The show was essentially a children's programme, in which members of the public, usually but not always youngsters, wrote in requesting to have their ambition fulfilled and host Jimmy Saville attempted to make their dream come true. In this case, an old dear named May Booker wrote and asked if Jim could fix it for her to perform with Thin Lizzy. The boys gamely came on the show, and played

'Hollywood', with Darren Wharton playing second fiddle to Mrs Booker and her keyboard solo. Out of respect for the show's youthful clientele, Lynott replaced the lines, 'People out in Hollywood, they got a lot of class, see them strutting down the boulevard, trying to make a pass,' (or 'kicking ass' when he sang it live), with 'People out in Hollywood, they got a lot of style, see them strutting down the boulevard, for a while.' The line 'Nobody give a damn' made it past the censors though.

'No One Told Him' (Lynott 3:36)
An up-tempo pop-rocker, consisting of someone lamenting the state his friend is in following a split with his girlfriend. In fact, he didn't even know they had split up apparently, because 'no one told him', not even the girlfriend, who is now getting an earful from the friend about her lack of tact and decent humanity. It's quite melodic and good fun in its own way, but it's also definitely filler.

'Fats' (White, Lynott 4:02)
Since the band's metamorphosis into a full-on hard-rocking group, attention started to focus on individual songs and whether they are Lizzy-like or not. To a large extent, Lizzy-like songs came to be defined as songs that could be imagined on *Live And Dangerous*. Songs that did not fit that template started to be less acceptable, and 'Fats' is a prime example. Although the 'Fats' in question is name-checked as Fats Waller at one point, he's a fictionalised version. A lowdown, sleazy bass line played on a conventional bass, with Lynott's fretless Schecter laid on top making it a two-bass song, underpin a hymn in praise of a jazz club owner, a portly, sharp-dressed New Orleans dude, or maybe the proprietor of a prohibition-era Chicago speakeasy. Many have raised the opinion, quite understandably, that this song should have gone to Phil's solo album. It's as far from the world of hard rock as can be imagined, and therefore 'un-Lizzy-like'. But is it really? Lynott's lyrical back-catalogue has often referenced different aspects of his Afro-Caribbean parentage, from the cool urban vibe of 'Black Boys On The Corner', to the smooth funk of 'Showdown'. The laid-back calypso of 'Half-Caste', the borderline gospel of 'Downtown Sundown' and 'Dear Heart', and 'Dancing In The Moonlight's finger-snapping soul carried on the tradition, and this is just another step in that direction. As such, it's a logical link in the chain, rather than an eccentric sideline. Lynott's ever-gruffer vocals lend themselves to a kind of Louis Armstrong impression that is perhaps a bit cornier than it could be, but his admiration for the suave, spat-shod Fats and his (no doubt) leggy companion is well-observed. It's easy to visualise the rotund, serene kingpin, on his arm (or perhaps a step behind as he strolls through the crowds at his establishment), a tall, willowy accomplice with just the hint of a supercilious smile. 'I like the way her lipstick matches the carnation on his tux,' croons Lynott in heavy-lidded wonder, and one wonders if he is considering whether he followed the

right musical path after all. Furthermore, Wharton pulls off an absolute miracle of a piano solo, combining a rattlesnake crawl with joyous, virtuoso jazz. OK, having said all that, I grant you that the verse about Sigmund Freud is a total dodo.

'Mexican Blood' (Lynott 3:40)
Here is the obligatory western-themed song, this time about a Mexican bandit who carries out raids on the US side of the border, making him a wanted man. A US lawman comes looking for him, and as usual with these things, it doesn't end well, especially for the bandito's señorita. Some nice acoustic guitar intro goes into an ominous, almost martial sound with more imaginatively stunning drum work, plus a xylophone for some reason. It's a tragic tale but a pretty lightweight track.

'It's Getting Dangerous' (Gorham, Lynott 5:30)
Thumping timpanis at the beginning, then a 1980s synth pad with whispered vocals, almost branching into Dire Straits territory. Lynott actually plays a Roland bass synth on this track, which plays synth sounds using the bass guitar rather than a keyboard as a controller. Plenty of 1980s sounds come out of the woodwork on this one, to make it feel more up-to-date – of course, a few decades later it starts to sound a bit dated: the manically-fast hi-hat work is supplemented by electronic percussion highlights. The lyric describes an old friend who succumbs to the danger he always warned his friends about – hunger for power leads to isolation and the loss of friendships. This song is lyrically much deeper than the average, and should perhaps have benefitted from a better package; this one sadly gets a bit lost at the end of the album – there is no guitar solo at all, just some background work towards the end.

Associated material
'Trouble Boys' (Billy Murray 3:32)
Released as a single 31 July 1981 with another non-album song, 'Memory Pain', on the B-side, ostensibly as a teaser for the album. Sadly, due to its poor performance, only reaching no. 53 in the UK, 'Trouble Boys' was actually pulled from the final album set before release. Even in Ireland, where the band tended to fare better, it only reached no. 30 and of course did not trouble the US charts at all. An unusual choice for the band, it's pure rockabilly. Writer Billy Murray was actually a pseudonym for Billy Bremner, not the 1970s Leeds United football captain but a Scottish guitarist who played with Lulu and the Luvvers, Nick Lowe, Dave Edmunds and Rockpile amongst others. He wrote it while in the Dave Edmunds band, and it appeared on Edmunds' fourth album *Tracks On Wax 4* in 1978. A real foot-tapper, it tells the story of a hapless young man who takes his girlfriend to a dance, where she is unwillingly picked up by a member of a large local gang of hell-raisers. He has a choice: let him take her away unchallenged, or stand up to the Trouble Boys – well what would you do?

'Memory Pain' (Percy Mayfield 4:44)

Released as the B-side to non-album track 'Trouble Boys', this blues number was written by American singer Percy Mayfield, best remembered as the writer of Ray Charles' classic 'Hit The Road Jack'. As such it is a pretty unusual choice for Lizzy, especially released on the reverse of another non-original song. 'Memory Pain' is a minor-key slow blues with a distinctive bass and guitar riff; it takes no effort at all to imagine it being performed by Peter Green's Fleetwood Mac. Snowy White is in his blues element here; it should be remembered that he deputised on guitar for the mentally befuddled Green on his comeback album *In The Skies,* on which Green wrote the songs and sang, but White played most of the guitar work. It may not be classic Lizzy, but it's a great blues piece.

'Girls' (Robertson, Bain, Lynott 4:01)

Serving as the B-Side to 'Hollywood (Down On Your Luck)' on the Canadian release only, this commercial, synth-heavy pop song is actually a Lynott solo song from *Solo In Soho*. Jimmy Bain played the piano and other keys, and drums were contributed by Californian Bob C. Benberg from Supertramp, who was also Scott Gorham's brother-in-law at the time. Backing vocals were served by a crew named Sophie, Margi, Silver, Christine and Lena, none of whom, apparently, had surnames – apart from Silver Smith. She was the ex-girlfriend of AC/DC frontman Bon Scott, who had died in 1980, apparently the day after ringing her up to ask her out again and being refused. On a lighter note, but not much lighter, the song serves as a kind of follow-up to 'Dear Miss Lonely Hearts', but this time a young woman writes to the agony aunt bemoaning her unrequited love for some nameless fellow. Of course, we are left to assume that she is the object of the misguided youth's affection from the 'Lonely Hearts' track, and thus the tragedy comes full circle – the newspaper columnist advises him to stay away from her, and her to stay away from him, possibly not connecting the two cases. Here is the lesson friends: do not let your lives be guided by newspaper columnists.

The Philip Lynott Album

Lynott's second solo album, released 17 September 1982. As with *Solo In Soho,* the recording took place against a backdrop of Thin Lizzy recording sessions, and again it wasn't all that clear which tracks would appear on which album until the final selection took place. The result was that every current member of Thin Lizzy appeared somewhere on the album, except for Snowy White – in fact, the only Lizzy guitarist of any era to appear apart from Scott Gorham was Midge Ure. This time though, no more than two Lizzy members appeared on any one song at the same time, so we will not be examining any specific track in detail. The most notable entry was a remix of the song 'Yellow Pearl', mentioned earlier. The album also included an ode to Lynott's second daughter with Caroline, the song named simply, 'Cathleen'.

Thunder And Lightning

Released: UK 4 March 1983, US 13 April 1983
Label: UK Vertigo, US Warner Bros
Recorded at: Lombard Studios, Dublin, Ireland; Power Plant and Boathouse
Studios, London, UK, 1982
The band are credited by name and by photo, but not by instrument:
Brian Downey (Drums, percussion)
John Sykes (Guitars, backing vocals)
Philip Lynott (Bass guitar, vocals)
Scott Gorham (Guitars, backing vocals)
Darren Wharton (Keyboards, backing vocals)
Produced by: Thin Lizzy and Chris Tsangarides
Album duration: 41 minutes
Chart position: UK: 4, US: 159

Lynott's long-drawn-out, second solo album was eventually released in 1982, having been delayed so as not to conflict with the launch of *Renegade*. Snowy White's tenure ended at about the same time, and Lynott went shopping again. This time there was no messing about with tact and taste; Gorham's new partner was a young, blond-maned axe-slinger with heavy metal shredder credentials. John Sykes had first dropped jaws with his unbelievably fast and fluid licks with Tygers Of Pan Tang; he was as fast as Gary Moore, and easier on the eye by some considerable margin. He also contributed to the writing on a couple of absolute heavy metal monster tracks on this set. No sooner had he appeared though, than the band started winding up business. The pressure and responsibility on Lynott's shoulders contributed to his drug habits, which in turn had effectively stopped normal functioning; he got up when he liked, worked when he liked and partied when he liked. Gorham was some way behind Lynott, but definitely on the same path. Even the rock-solid Downey was getting disillusioned with the whole thing. Thin Lizzy employed a permanent staff of over 30 people, but they were massively in debt, and the revolving door of guitarists and the rapid-fire changes in musical direction had sapped a degree of interest even amongst the faithful. Ticket sales had slowed to a crawl and the management had other bands to promote. There was only one thing for it, and that was to line up one last spectacular effort, throw everything at it and hope that it covered enough of the bills to appease their creditors. Thin Lizzy announced that this next album would be their last and the attached tour would be farewell.

The tour started in the UK in February 1983 and with a definite schedule in mind, due to end at the 1983 Reading Festival in the UK – but it sold out almost immediately, and suddenly it seemed as if the debts could be recouped after all. So more and more dates were added and the tour never seemed to come to an end. Brian Downey told the author in conversation:

John Sykes really kind of saved the band at the end of the day when he came in. The tour was kind of a farewell tour and I think we had a month, maybe two months pencilled in, but that whole tour went on for over a year in the end.

In so doing, it also yielded another double-live album, a swan song named *Life*; more of that later.

Album cover

Lynott reportedly demanded a gatefold sleeve against stiff opposition from the label, and ended up getting one; in the UK the album was released as a limited edition gatefold with a bonus four-song 12" live 33rpm EP, showcasing four songs from the *Live At Hammersmith Odeon* set featuring Snowy White – the songs included were 'Emerald', 'Killer On The Loose', 'The Boys Are Back In Town' and 'Hollywood (Down On Your Luck)', although test pressings exist with 'Waiting For An Alibi' instead of 'Emerald'. Jim Fitzpatrick designed a spectacular cover with a semi-abstract design depicting a fist tightly grasping a bolt of searing lightning against a background of stars, but it was declined by the record company. Instead, they went for a cheaper option that has been derided, even ridiculed by fans as a cheap knock-off, but to be honest, it's still spectacular – it's just a long way from anything ever before seen on a Thin Lizzy album and it's overtly heavy metal. A guitar juts out of the ground on the horizon, semi-silhouetted against a glowering sky. It is struck by a thunderbolt from the clouds, as a leather-clad and metal-studded fist punches its way out of the blasted gravel in the foreground. A zoomed-in extract of the same picture appears on the back along with the tracklisting and a live photo of the band. The inside of the gatefold is entirely taken up with a panoramic shot of all five members, with Darren Wharton getting in on the scene at last. Lynott is clearly looking for a passive-aggressive image at this point; his hand encased in a vicious Rollerball-themed metal-studded glove holding, incongruously, a bright green apple, perhaps advertising him as an original sinner, or perhaps just giving him an excuse to brandish that vicious-looking glove.

'Thunder And Lightning' (Downey, Lynott 4:56)

Released as a pretty confusing second album single in April 1983; A single edit of this song, running as 45rpm, was issued with an edited live version of 'Still In Love With You' on the B-side (recorded at Hammersmith Odeon on 10 March 1983), which ran at 33rpm. This unlikely combination reached no. 39 in the UK. Production of that live take was credited to Darren Wharton, although Lynott has gone on record as saying it should have been joint-credited to Wharton, John Sykes and Will Reid-Dick (who had served in an engineering capacity on-and-off since *Johnny The Fox*). In any case, 'Thunder And Lightning' kicks off the album with a synthesized crash of thunder, then a heavy riff that goes into a powerful, driving force of a track. It's immediately clear that Lizzy are taking a new direction with this set, as this is far and away the hardest, most driving power rock they ever produced. The vocals are fast and frenetic, and almost like shouted rap, purging the frustration of a schoolkid bent on cutting loose at the weekend. There are loads of harmonies and steaming guitars, but it's three minutes in before we get to hear what John Sykes is made of with the first solo proper. We have all heard a lot about vocals that glorify violence, but this piece literally does, describing getting into a Saturday night fight down the club with relish and adrenalin-fuelled detail. Aptly, it finishes on another crash of thunder.

'This Is the One' (Wharton, Lynott 4:04)
Squealing guitars set the scene under a percussive, power-chord backing. The verses are growled rather than sung, over a repetitive ticking rhythm. The first couple of verses are a pretty good description of Lynott's brain-addled, soporific state, although there is optimism in the chorus as if the culmination of some great enterprise is approaching. The answer-back solo is exciting, with Gorham in the right channel and Sykes on the left, the power chords drive the song along, but the metronomic rhythm doesn't escalate and the track doesn't really go anywhere. The main ingredient that is missing is melody – the guitars have completely left the sing-song harmonies behind.

'The Sun Goes Down' (Wharton, Lynott 6:20)
Released as a single in cut-down 4:20 format in July 1983 with 'Baby Please Don't Go' on the B-side; a remixed version was also released on 12". The third single from the album, it was also the least successful at a UK peak position of no. 52. In what could basically considered a bit of poor album planning, this number utilises essentially the same ticking rhythm as the last one, but on rim-shot rather than snare. It's not the same song by any means, but it might have been a better idea to separate them a little more. Bubbling keyboards pile on the desolation and it's atmospheric for sure, with ambient guitar chords that pan rapidly left and right and washes of warm keyboard pad. Gorham stumps up a screaming, reverb-soaked solo. This one is all about the atmosphere; the 'demon among us' at the beginning becomes the 'demon within us' by the end, with Lynott almost whispering underneath ominous keyboard passages.

'The Holy War' (Lynott 5:12)
The demon of the last song is replaced with the actual devil in this pseudo-religious anthem, which makes direct reference to Satan's temptations of Christ. Although the song is based on religious conflict and confusion, with the moral that no one wins a holy war, Lynott's Catholic upbringing stands out in sharp relief. The gothic imagery is dark and heavy, with almost Dracula overtones; Lynott personifies the religious warlord at one point, laying down the law in stern tones with a female voice muttering heartfelt invocations, really quietly in the background. It's much heavier than the previous song, but there's an uncomfortable feeling by now that the band is more or less going

through the motions – the songs don't escalate or progress, they set out their stall at the beginning and play themselves to an inevitable fadeout. It doesn't help that electronic drum sounds are starting to bleed in from the musical desert that was 1980s popular music.

'Cold Sweat' (Sykes, Lynott 3:06)

Well, this one at least rocks hard and heavy. It was the album's lead single, released on 4 February 1983 with 'Bad Habits' on the B-side. It reached no. 27 in the UK, the most successful of the album's three singles. This combo also hit the streets as a double-disc single, with live versions of 'Angel Of Death' and 'Don't Believe A Word' (recorded at Hammersmith Odeon on 27 November 1981) on the bonus disc; this four-song combination was also released as a 12" single. A John Sykes heavy metal workout kicks off each side of the LP, with this full-on finger-tapping metal anthem firing the starting gun for side two. With a backing riff worthy of Saxon, Judas Priest or – more likely – Tygers Of Pan Tang, the band were dipping their toes into the New Wave Of British Heavy Metal here. A thudding, rumbling bass, shredding guitars and a driving rhythm form the backing for a serious warning concerning the dangers of a gambling addiction; this could almost be a follow-up to 'Waiting For An Alibi'. A tight power-chord ending brings it to a juddering stop. A lot of fans cite this as a highlight of the entire catalogue, which it certainly is if you're a fan of Saxon, Judas Priest or Tygers Of Pan Tang, but if 'Fats' was too soft and fluffy, then 'Cold Sweat' was arguably just as much of a swing in the opposite direction. It's a memorable metal anthem without doubt, if somewhat derivative. Gorham for one, much as he lived the rock'n'roll lifestyle, is known to have hated the whole 'heavy metal' image. This song was also resurrected in 1991 as the B-side to the 'Dedication' single release.

'Someday She Is Going To Hit Back' (Downey, Wharton, Lynott 4:05)

Another thunderclap to start, more realistic this time. Power chords and warbling sci-fi keyboard sounds presage the coming storm; then a rapid drum riff leads into a fast pop-rock anthem. Probably one of the most underrated and undervalued tracks in the whole Lizzy repertoire, it's fantastically put together, veering into prog-fusion territory. The guitar and keyboard solos are blisteringly fast, with harmonies thrown in, but it's a massive wall of juggernaut sound. The words are almost completely indecipherable underneath layers of instrumentation and backing vocals, which may be partly why it tends to pass under the radar, but lyrically it is a statement that no one is going to let themselves be oppressed or bullied forever, however vulnerable they may appear. At the three-minute mark, I kid you not, there is a section in 11/8 time. Originally demoed under the title 'Woman Don't Like It', this is a thundering freight train of a track, and yet another direction the band could have taken.

'Baby Please Don't Go' (Lynott 5:10)

This made it to the B-side of 'The Sun Goes Down' in July 1983. Another fast pop-rock song, much clearer and more accessible than the last one, opening with a strident guitar line. Sykes, somewhat incongruously, throws in some squeaking guitar and whammy-bar riffage, but there is catchy melody in amongst the rock, and some seriously great soloing.

'Bad Habits' (Gorham, Lynott 4:04)

OK, it really looked for a while as if Thin Lizzy were going to go out with a thunderous roar, but just to show they are the same old band, they have included the obligatory silly sexual one. The song has more melody than on the rest of the album admittedly, but it's really just a throwaway piece of fluff. Lynott lusts after everyone passing by, which he admits is a 'bad habit', but the band accompanies it with a jolly, swinging rhythm – until a minute and a half, when it suddenly drops back into hard rock for a few bars before some sweet guitar work in a straight major key pulls it back into fluffy territory. For some reason, this song was selected as the B-side to 'The Sun Goes Down' on some copies of the Dutch release.

'Heart Attack' (Wharton, Gorham, Lynott 3:39)

Another heavy pop-rocker; Thin Lizzy go melodic metal in the vein of Thunder, Whitesnake or Bon Jovi. It's a well-constructed piece with a hard, tight ending, but considering it turned out to be the last song on the band's final studio album, one would have to say that its repeated strain of 'Mama, I'm dying, oh Papa, I'm dying, dying, dying, dying,' is pretty poignant.

Associated Material
'Don't Let It Slip Away' (Lynott 8:08)

This rare song is usually billed as 'Don't Let Him Slip Away', depending on the source, the version and the exact lyrics Lynott chose to sing at the time. Starting as another downbeat ballad in the vein of 'The Sun Goes Down' but building into a power-chord juggernaut, this one sadly didn't make the cut, perhaps partly at least because of its length. It may also have been considered somewhat too similar to some of the other material with its 'demon that lives in the fire' baroque sensibilities. Musically speaking, it might have been worth ditching two other tracks to include this worthy epic. You might pick any two out of 'The Sun Goes Down', 'Holy War' and 'This Is The One' perhaps. It could have been faded out at least half a minute early as nothing happens in those final 30 seconds, but it probably went on the flip of a coin in the end. If you feel the need to track it down, two alternative takes appear on the massive bootleg compilation *Phil Lynott: The Man And His Music*.

Life (Live)

Released: UK 16 November 1983, also released in US
Label: UK Vertigo, US Warner Bros
Recorded at: Hammersmith Odeon, London, UK, 10-12 March 1983
Philip Lynott: Lead vocals, bass guitar
Brian Downey: drums, percussion, backing vocals
Scott Gorham: Lead and harmony guitars, backing vocals
Darren Wharton: Keyboards, backing vocals
John Sykes: Lead and harmony guitars, backing vocals
Snowy White: Lead and harmony guitars (on Renegade)
Guest appearances:
Gary Moore, Eric Bell, Brian Robertson: Guitars
Produced by: Phil Lynott and Thin Lizzy
Album duration: 98 minutes
Chart position: UK: 29, US: 185

Well, it was inevitable that the farewell tour would generate a farewell live album, but it was always likely to be bitter-sweet. Lizzy were predominantly a live band, with a reputation for ferocious live shows that was laid on the table with *Live And Dangerous.* It seemed unlikely that the same atmosphere could be recaptured, but the band had a lot more catalogue to play with, and the prospect of chugging out some of the later, hard-rocking material was enticing. John Sykes was the guitarist-in-residence partnering Scott Gorham, but the band pulled out all the stops by drafting in as many previous guitarists as they could get hold of. Eric Bell, Brian Robertson and Gary Moore all step onstage, and at the finale, they all come on together in a feast of axe-slinging nostalgia. Some older recordings from the Snowy White era are also included, although he does not appear in the finale.

In an interview with Neil Jeffries for *Kerrang* magazine at the time, Lynott described the layout of the album:

It's presented differently with the band as it stands now with John, the modern stuff, on side one. Then side two will be the lighter stuff, including a couple of Snowy's things. On side three we're gonna have the 'hit singles', then the last side is like, 'the epics' – 'Emerald', 'Black Rose', 'Still In Love With You' and 'The Rocker'. Most of it consists of songs since Live And Dangerous, because that album was such a milestone in our career, some people forget we did a lot after it as well!

As it happens, the originally-planned last gig of all on this tour, at the Reading Festival in August 1983, was also recorded by the BBC. This remained unreleased, however, until September 1992, when it eventually saw daylight as the 77-minute set *Thin Lizzy Live: BBC Radio 1 Live In Concert.*

Album Cover

A bright blue gatefold sleeve sports a variation of Jim Fitzpatrick's 'Thin Lizzy' logo in huge lettering at the top, with an uncredited photo of Lynott on stage, silhouetted in front of a misty spotlight, underneath. The album title *Life* is picked out at the bottom in a lighter blue, with a yellow 'V' superimposed over the 'F', so that the word can be read either as 'Life' or 'Live'. In the same interview with *Kerrang* magazine, Lynott drew a comparison between this album title and the whole Tin Lizzie vs Thin Lizzy Irish accent pronunciation scenario:

> I thought it was a good play on words – when you go into the record shop and say, 'Can I have the Thin Lizzy Life album?' That's what the name 'Thin' is all about – Tin Lizzie – the Irish accent thing!

The back cover has a stage shot of one of the actual gigs, with eight band members on stage: Moore and Sykes on the far left, Downey mostly hidden behind his drumkit, Lynott at the mic, with Gorham, Robertson and Bell lined up on the right. Wharton is out of shot. The tracklisting is in loud, yellow lettering, with much smaller print crediting virtually everyone who has ever been involved with the band, accountants, roadies, techs, publicists, artists and photographers amongst others, even historical support bands.

The inside cover is also a potted history of the band, with photos of all the current members taken on the tour, plus older monochrome and promo shots. Most notable perhaps, is a great shot of Dave Flett and Midge Ure, both briefly members of the band during the *Black Rose* tour, both sporting guitars and both grinning widely.

'Thunder And Lightning' (from *Thunder And Lightning* 5:11)

Starts with a crash of thunder coming in over the crowd, then that familiar 'Jailbreak' opening power chord. It's a brave starter, full-on and as heavy as it will get all night, a direct facsimile of the studio version. The backing is a little muffled, but the solos are clear, and the thunder crash ending is perfectly executed.

'Waiting For An Alibi' (from *Black Rose* 3:16)

A lovely, greasy bass intro; Lynott's laconic, sleepy vocal delivery seems to be a bit behind the music a lot of the time, but the harmony guitars are spot on, including the final note...

'Jailbreak' (from *Jailbreak* 4:08)

That slowed-down, atmospheric final riff of the previous track is not left to hang for long, as the band launch straight into a rapid version of 'Jailbreak'. At last, Lynott says a few words to the crowd to get them going just before the police siren section, and then a bit more afterwards, but there has been no audience chatting yet! Still lazy and laconic, Lynott's voice is gruff and is already starting to sound a bit tired, as if he has been singing for hours.

'Baby Please Don't Go' (from *Thunder And Lightning* 5:02)
A great, hard-rocking version of this melodic rocker, but Sykes' solo is buried deep for the first half until someone eventually bumps up the slider on his channel. There is some fearsome, thudding bass towards the end and the whole thing rocks along at a blistering lick, with a blasting crash ending.

'Holy War' (from *Thunder And Lightning* 4:53)
Lynott starts straight into the introductory repetitive bass note, accompanied by drums that thankfully miss the 1980s tinny timbre of the studio version. It's a rocking version of this song, very fast, with super-tight backing vocals and a nice solo from Sykes. A perfectly-executed harmony note ends a great track.

'Renegade' (from *Renegade* 6:15)
The first ballad of the set is chosen to kick off side two of the vinyl, but it's notable that this is not from the same set, the same tour or even the same year. Lynott starts with solo bass accompanied by the audience clapping along until the band comes in on a beautifully mixed subtle guitar and drum combo. And yes, it's Snowy White, even though he is conspicuously missing from the guest musicians list and the photos. It doesn't sound out of place in the set, but the sound is actually miles better if you listen out for it. An excellent rendition.

'Hollywood Down On Your Luck' (from *Renegade* 4:10)
The previous number goes straight into this one without a break, so it's evidently still Snowy White, although he is only credited on the album for the one track. Lynott's voice is noticeably clearer and he sounds more awake and more alive. The guitars are definitely coming through better as well.

'Got To Give It Up' (from *Black Rose* 7:05)
At last, Lynott gives it a bit of that old Irish blarney and presents a mock Big-Brother monologue for a minute and a half before this next song. The audience joins in singing the opening bars over an atmospheric Pink Floyd-style start; in fact, it's almost a pastiche. The number proper doesn't come in until nearly two and a half minutes, hence the apparent seven-minute track length. It's not too fast or too loud, though; it's a perfect rendition and certainly the best-executed song so far, from the Sykes material at least. An extended Sykes solo at the end is clear as a bell as the sound seems to be improving.

'Angel Of Death' (from *Renegade* 5:56)
For some reason, they decided to completely leave out Wharton's atmospheric keyboard build-up and go straight into the thudding, galloping bass line. He gets a great solo in the middle, though, which the audience evidently appreciates.

'Are You Ready' (from *Live And Dangerous* 3:00)

The previous track launches straight into this one, the first actual driving rocker of the set so far, with some steamingly fast drum breaks and a huge crash ending to finish side two.

'The Boys Are Back In Town' (from *Jailbreak* 4:53)

Side three of the vinyl fades in on Lynott doing his 'No! no!' routine, reminiscent of the intro to encore 'The Rocker' on *Live And Dangerous*. Then, *apropos* of nothing, he throws in the phrase, 'It's the life for me', which is the cue for a well-practised version of this song, with crystal clear backing vocals.

'Cold Sweat' (from *Thunder And Lightning* 3:08)

Good rocking version of this metal workout, pretty well exactly as per the studio version – except for the fact that Lynott can't say 'Stone cold sober and stone cold sweat' in the heat of the moment, so we get 'Cold stone sober and cold stone sweat' all the way through. Sykes nails the shredding and finger-tapping solo.

'Don't Believe A Word' (from *Johnny The Fox* 5:12)

A chorus-soaked ballad intro starts up, with Lynott saying this is 'an old song with the original arrangement.' The ambient, bluesy version of this song always sounds great, and if it wasn't so brilliant as a rock track, it would seem that Lizzy missed a decent trick not doing it this way in the first place. Sykes' echo-laden and whammy bar-stoked solo is completely different from the Peter Green-influenced weeping blues of the Snowy White era, but it works well enough. At 3½ minutes it stops and goes abruptly into a chugging, single-chord shuffle for another minute and a half, but then stops on an outro of the familiar rock riff. Check out the version Lizzy did in the hour-long *Live At Hammersmith* set from November 1981, where they play the full rocking version at the end, which was even better.

'Killer On The Loose' (from *Chinatown* 4:59)

Surprisingly, this is the first song from *Chinatown* on this album. It's relatively restrained though, only starting to warm up a bit with the key change to the second (Gorham) solo. Lynott warms up the audience for a joyous 'Killer on the loose' singalong and a decent crash ending. The audience seems to love this one.

'The Sun Goes Down' (from *Thunder And Lightning* 6:45)

Starts with a gong, which sounds a bit wimpy in truth. Rim-shots and loads of atmospheric keyboards underpin pan-bouncing vocal echoes. Gorham executes a great, echo-laden solo.

'Emerald' (from *Jailbreak* 3:26)

Strangely, the final note of the previous song had not finished fading out when a knife-and-fork bit of editing has Lynott promising to bring out Brian

Robertson, Gary Moore, Eric Bell and 'me mother.' Then another hatchet job cuts to him saying simply, 'Emerald,' and we're away. This number rocks hard as always and features Robbo doing a guest spot, to massive applause.

'Black Rose' (from *Black Rose* 6:40)
The audience cheers fade out and this track is laid on over the top. Sykes and Moore play 'Danny Boy' in unison; both play the answerbacks in 'The Mason's Apron', which, as you might expect, is impressively but manically rapid. A lovely, melodic ending replaces the studio version's fadeout.

'Still In Love With You' (from *Nightlife* 8:58)
This is even slower than and just as atmospheric as the *Live And Dangerous* version. Sykes plays probably his best solo on the album, following Robbo's famous first solo from *Live And Dangerous* almost note for note, with his own flourishes thrown in. Gorham's closing solo is at least as good as his one on *L&D* and the ending is perfect.

'The Rocker' (from *Vagabonds Of The Western World* 4:50)
Eric Bell opens with his distinctive guitar tone, treble-rich and somewhat tinny. It's pure nostalgia to hear him launching into his old solo. At the end, Lynott counts all the musicians off as they all join in a strident rocking riff in unison: Bell, Gorham, Moore, Robertson, Sykes, Wharton, Downey. An ecstatic audience tries its best to drown out the band at the huge, career-concluding crash ending.

Associated material
'Out In The Fields' (Gary Moore 4:18)
Gary Moore had had a massive hit with 'Parisienne Walkways' in 1979, with lyrics by Lynott, who also sang and played bass, and Brian Downey guesting on drums. This was a kind of a reprise of that success, on Moore's 1985 album *Run For Cover*, except that the drums were provided by ex-Roxy Music drummer Paul Thompson. Although a Moore-penned song, it was a true collaboration with Moore and Lynott sharing the vocals and also the sleeve photo, in vintage-style red military coats. The single was even credited to 'Gary Moore and Phil Lynott'. The theme of the song is usually given as the troubles in Northern Ireland, and indeed there are some reflections of that conflict in the lyrics, but it seems to be more wide-ranging than that, condemning the futility and irrationality of any bloody conflict based on political or religious ideology. Amazingly, its success eclipsed even 'Parisienne Walkways', reaching no. 5 in the UK chart, being the highest-charting single ever released by either Lynott or Moore, either solo or in bands. The B-side was another song from the same album, 'Military Man', sung by Lynott. Again, both songs regularly appear on 'Best of Phil Lynott and Thin Lizzy' type compilations. Sadly, the single's success did Lynott little good; it was one of the last recordings he ever made but was a glorious swan song.

'Military Man' (Lynott, Laurence Archer, Mark Stanway 5:40)

From Gary Moore's album *Run For Cover,* this song was released as the B-side to 'Out In The Fields' – but originally it was neither a Gary Moore nor Thin Lizzy song, originating in Lynott's Grand Slam project. In fact a six-minute version eventually appeared on a 2002 collection of their recordings named *Grand Slam: Studio Sessions.* Writer's credits variously appear as Lynott, Lynott/Stanway or Lynott/Archer/Stanway.

'Dedication' (Lynott, Laurence Archer 4:00)

Released as a single 14 January 1991 with 'Cold Sweat' on the B-side and reaching no. 35 in the UK (and a tremendous no. 2 in Ireland, the band's most successful single there since 'Don't Believe A Word' in 1976), this fabulous melodic metal piece is about as contentious as it gets. It was written by Grand Slam guitarist Laurence Archer, by his own account, when he was in one of his previous bands named Stampede. Grand Slam recorded a demo, but it was never released. However, when Phonogram released a compilation Thin Lizzy album in 1991, they not only dug up this track and marketed it as an unreleased Lizzy track, but they used it in the title for the album *Dedication: The Very Best of Thin Lizzy, and* released it as a single *and* replaced Archer's writer's credits with Lynott. There are several parallel realities about this song doing the rounds, including the assertion that Lynott wrote the song and did the original take himself with just bass and vocals, with Downey and Gorham adding the drum and guitar parts prior to this release. However, the most popular and widely-distributed account is that Archer did in fact play the guitar on the original demo, but that his guitar part was discarded and Downey and Gorham added drums and guitars, adding a final twist of the knife in Archer's back. According to Mark Putterford in his book *The Rocker*, Gary Moore was also invited to take part and started working on the song, but the single was released in the meantime, regardless, without any input from him at all. Archer took legal action and was eventually reinstated as a co-writer at least. Further spice is added by the alternative stories that the guitar work on the finished piece is, in fact, Archer's (certainly Gorham's lead guitar style had moved on from his Thin Lizzy days, with a smoother tone and some added whammy bar), or that Archer played guitar and bass on the demo, and that even if the guitar is not his, the bass probably is. To be honest, the more people you speak to about it, the more different accounts you will get.

The video usually associated with the piece, (all over YouTube for instance), shows the Robertson/Gorham incarnation of the band, quite clearly playing a different song completely. In fact it's more than one song, as Robertson's guitar keeps changing, with the recording of 'Dedication' laid loosely over the top. All of which is a thorough shame, because it really is a great song, definitely in the 1980s glam metal genre – think of the Sammy Hagar era of Van Halen or Whitesnake at their most commercial. Grand Slam eventually reformed in 2016, and in 2018 recorded their first actual, official album, named *Hit The Ground*. 'Dedication' was re-recorded and included on the record, and arguably found its true home at last, although sadly without Lynott's vocals.

What Phil did next...

Thin Lizzy played their final gig on 4 September 1983 in Nuremberg, Germany, at the *Monsters Of Rock* festival. Plenty of bands have played 'final gigs' and gone on to reform 'due to popular demand', and this could have happened to Lizzy, but unfortunately, Phil Lynott's life was unravelling faster than he could scoop it back up. Scott Gorham took advantage of the break to clear up his drug habit, but Lynott's got worse if anything; his marriage broke up and he was left flailing. He did the only thing he knew how to do – he started another band. This was the aforementioned Grand Slam, originally with Downey on drums, Sykes on guitar and Mark Stanway from Magnum on keys, who had played in Lynott's solo touring band. This line-up folded almost immediately, though, with Sykes accepting an invitation to join Whitesnake and Downey pulling out on the grounds of musical integrity – as he explained to the author:

> I decided not to go ahead with it in the end because I just found the band was so shambolic and unrehearsed, I kind of got cold feet. We were on the verge of an Irish tour and we just didn't have the set together at all. The tour was smallish bars, they weren't proper venues at all, and Phil had the idea of doing the tour to get the band tight. But I just thought it was the wrong decision, because we weren't tight, the rehearsals proved that to me. Phil was turning up six, seven hours late, which was crazy, and we did not have a proper set together, there were only a few days to go and I said look, we have to cancel this tour. Compared to Thin Lizzy, this is an absolute shambles.

Nevertheless, the tour went ahead with a hastily-rehearsed Robbie Brennan replacing Downey on drums and Laurence Archer and Doish Nagle on guitars, but they never landed a record deal and played their last gig in December 1984. Lynott branched out into diverse ventures, mentoring younger bands promulgating folk and soul, recording solo, collaborating on Gary Moore's solo output and working with Huey Lewis and The News just before they really started making it big. For the last few years of his life, he was working on a project with a Dublin folk group named Clann Éadair. He wrote and recorded a song named 'A Tribute to Sandy Denny' with them, appeared with them when they performed it on Irish TV, and he was working on producing their album right down to the end. Lynott's last single was named 'Nineteen', produced by electronic pop pioneer Paul Hardcastle, who also had a massive hit with a different song named '19'. Sadly though, Lynott's star was setting fast.

Philip Parris Lynott collapsed on Christmas day 1985 and was taken to Salisbury infirmary, where he died on 4 January 1986, officially of heart failure and septicaemia secondary to pneumonia, but effectively as a direct result of the massive, ongoing, toxic results of heroin addiction. His funeral was held in Richmond on 9th and he is buried at St. Fintan's cemetery on the outskirts of Dublin. He was 36.

A life-size bronze statue of Lynott by sculptor Paul Daly was erected in Harry

Street in Dublin in 2005. Since 1987, a music festival named the *Vibe For Philo* has been held in Lynott's honour in Dublin every year on the anniversary of his death. It always includes Thin Lizzy tribute bands and often ex-band members and even reformed line-ups of bands associated with Lynott. His mother Philomena was an enthusiastic supporter of the festival and of any and all fans of her son's music until her death from lung cancer in 2019 at the age of 88. She is also buried at St. Fintan's.

What the rest did next...

There is no doubt that Thin Lizzy was associated primarily with its charismatic frontman, singer, bassist and main writer Phil Lynott. When he died, the whole image apparently went with him. Nevertheless, there was life in it yet.

The members had all gone their separate ways. Eric Bell had joined Noel Redding from the Jimi Hendrix Experience in his band for a while after leaving Lizzy, then went on to record with his own Eric Bell Band.

Original keyboardist Bob Wrixon gradually gravitated back to Them after leaving the embryonic Thin Lizzy, and died in 2015.

John Du Cann, who had partnered Andy Gee on tour after Bell left, had a top 40 hit single with a song called 'Don't Be A Dummy' in 1979, which was used on a TV advert for Levi's jeans, then re-formed Atomic Rooster for a while. He recorded a solo album in 1977 which was eventually released in 1992 and he died of a heart attack in 2011.

Andy Gee did session work and played with a number of obscure bands before a radical genre switch to house music in the 1990s.

Scott Gorham joined Phenomena II before he and bassist Leif Johansen went off to form 21 Guns.

Brian Robertson formed Wild Horses with Jimmy Bain in 1980, thereafter joining heavy metal monsters Motörhead, whose live Birthday Party video in 1985 included a guest appearance by Phil Lynott. Since then, Robbo's foot never seemed to find a comfortable place to rest, as he guested on varied and disparate projects.

Midge Ure became an electronic pop pioneer in bands such as Visage (which was formed before his brief tenure in Thin Lizzy) and Ultravox.

Dave Flett, who joined Lizzy briefly while Midge was playing the keyboards, formed Special Branch and also guested with Lizzy on the *Renegade* tour.

Gary Moore played with Jon Hiseman's Colosseum II, did one album with Jack Bruce and Ginger Baker as BBM (Baker Bruce Moore), in which he basically took over from Eric Clapton in a reformed Cream, and brought out a string of excellent solo rock albums before discovering a new direction as the world's predominant blues guitarist. Moore died of a heart attack in Spain in 2011 at the age of 58.

Darren Wharton formed and fronted his own band named Dare.

John Sykes was briefly with Whitesnake before forming his own band Blue Murder, in which he was guitarist, frontman and songwriter. When they were dropped by their label, Sykes recorded under his own name.

Snowy White released a string of solo albums starting with *White Flames* in 1983, which featured his melodic, whimsical ballad 'Bird Of Paradise', which became a UK top 10 hit single.

Brian Downey's output was largely with Lizzy-related bands, playing on albums by Sykes and Gary Moore and others.

Mark Nauseef, the only other drummer besides Downey ever to occupy Lizzy's drum stool, went on to play with everyone, his CV reflecting a genuine

Who's Who of the rock world, including Gary Moore's G-Force and Lynott's two solo albums. His tenure with Lizzy included the famous Sydney Harbour gig in 1978 when Downey was briefly on hiatus.

Ten years after Lynott's demise, the remaining members of Thin Lizzy's last line-up reformed to keep alive the music and the legacy. John Sykes took on the lead vocals, as he had done with his own band Blue Murder. Scott Gorham, Brian Downey and Darren Wharton all signed up, along with Blue Murder's bassist Marco Mendoza. Downey left soon afterwards, and in 2000 the band recorded a single live album of existing Lizzy material named *One Night Only* with Whitesnake drummer Tommy Aldridge on board.

The band continued on-and-off for the next decade with various line-ups, always including Sykes and Gorham, until Sykes left for good in 2009. With only Gorham left to carry the flag, he reformed the band again in late 2009, pulling off a coup by getting Brian Downey and Darren Wharton back, as well as recruiting Alice Cooper guitarist Damon Johnson. The vacant singer spot was filled by Northern Irishman Ricky Warwick, whose most high-profile work beforehand had been with Scottish rockers The Almighty. As Lizzy were now effectively a Lizzy tribute band, Warwick had one job, which was to sound as much like Phil Lynott as possible, a task which he fulfilled admirably, even if he looked nothing like him.

Inevitably, as the band started to pull together, and with writers on board in the shape of Warwick and Johnson, they considered releasing some original material, keeping closely to the Lizzy Gaelic-rock template. However, both the band and a proportion of the fans felt that Thin Lizzy without Phil Lynott was not Thin Lizzy at all and that they should change the band name, so they settled on the title Black Star Riders. As it happened though, the prospect of starting out on a massive tour schedule with a new band didn't sit that well with Downey, who was already in comfortable semi-retirement in Ireland, so he pulled out of the new project. Wharton too, having fronted his own band, was not keen to sit in the background and left to concentrate on Dare. So the new band, with its full-on Thin Lizzy sound, was not only *not* Thin Lizzy, but only included one member from the Lynott days in Scott Gorham. Ironically their first single, 'Bound For Glory' in March 2013, could not have sounded more like Lizzy if it had been Lizzy. It was all there; the Irish musical phrasing, the harmony guitars, and a singer who sounded more like Phil than Phil did.

Black Star Riders only gradually moved away from their roots, developing their own sound and image. The Thin Lizzy line-up still parades out from time to time; the 2016 Ramblin' Man Fair rock festival in Maidstone, Kent included both Thin Lizzy and Black Star Riders on the same bill, a real treat for Lizzy fans – and Gorham fans in particular!

Incidentally, Brian Downey eventually formed a stunning nostalgia-fest of a band named Brian Downey's Alive And Dangerous, playing a Thin Lizzy repertoire made up predominantly (but not exclusively) of numbers from *Live and Dangerous*.

Compilation Albums

Strangely enough, Thin Lizzy compilation albums were few and far between during the active years. None of the three original Decca albums troubled the charts at all, and even after the band started getting recognition at Vertigo, Decca were a bit slack at marketing their back catalogue. Even Vertigo didn't start stumping up any collections until the band had already lost traction in America and had started to decline in Europe. Nevertheless, the stream started flowing eventually, so the list below doesn't even attempt to list every compilation, but hopefully pulls out the most notable examples, which either made a decent showing in the charts or presented previously-unreleased material...

Remembering Part 1

In cases such as this, where a band is dropped by one label but then finds fame and fortune with another, the usual practice is for the original label to trot out endless compilations of their old material in the hope that the record-buying public won't realise they are getting prototype music. In the wake of *Jailbreak's* success, Decca dusted off Lizzy's back catalogue and selected ten numbers to showcase the old ways. They managed to get this 41-minute compilation out in August 1976, a couple of months ahead of *Johnny The Fox* and they even engaged Jim Fitzpatrick to create another 'Cosmic Cowboy' style cover, with a stern-faced Lynott on his Rocker space-bike bursting out of the frame in explosions of fire, and Downey making the peace sign from the pillion – Eric Bell is following on a separate bike, with Gary Moore in the distance like the fourth biker of the apocalypse. Although non-canonical, it's worth listing the tracks, which included some singles, B-sides and rarities, making it actually pretty indispensable to completists at the time. In the US and Canada, a very similar compilation was issued named *The Rocker 1971-1974,* containing all the same tracks except that 'A Song For While I'm Away' was replaced with 'Honesty Is No Excuse' for reasons best known to the stateside distributor London Records. It didn't use the Fitzpatrick cover either. All of these tracks would later reappear on CD editions of the various albums, but at the time of writing this book, this compilation itself had never been released on CD except in the US in 1998.

'Black Boys On The Corner' (3:22): Previously only available on single, this was the first time the song appeared on an official album, although it would later see daylight on expanded versions of both *Orphanage* and *Vagabonds*.

'A Song for While I'm Away' (5:08): From *Vagabonds Of The Western World,* this is as per the original.

'Randolph's Tango' (3:45): Previously only available on single, although this is not the 7" single 2:25 version but a previously-unreleased full-length edition. Both versions would later appear on the 2010 expanded CD edition of *Vagabonds*.

'Little Girl In Bloom' (3:46): Originally from *Vagabonds,* but this version is rather hurriedly faded out at a quiet bit, sadly omitting Bell's luminous and joyful solo at the end lasting nearly a minute and a half, with its previews of the classic harmonising guitars to come.

'Sitamoia' (3:25): A bit difficult to know where to put this one; it was recorded during Gary Moore's first tenure with the band after Eric Bell's departure, so was included in the 'Associated material' section of *Vagabonds*, but in actual fact it never saw the light of day until *Remembering Part 1*. So this one was a real rarity at the time, and is credited to Lynott as the sole writer – in most other places it is attributed to Downey.

'Little Darling' (2:55): Another song from the first Gary Moore era, this rarity was previously only known from its single release in April 1974, when it pretty much sank like a stone.

'Remembering' (4:00): Originally from the band's self-titled first album, this version like 'Little Girl In Bloom' takes advantage of a quiet bit to just stop and launch, quite imaginatively, straight into the next track. Thus we lose two minutes of screaming psychedelic wig-out on two lead guitars, although it's pretty much the same fare as the existing solo, so there might be some justification in truncating it...

'Gonna Creep Up On You' (3:25): ... especially as the segue to the beginning of this track is a masterpiece. Lynott vocalises an emotive 'Oh yeah' as 'Remembering' dives into its jazz fusion freeform section, and instead of giving us the whole nine yards of Bell's solo, it just cuts straight to the grimy, greasy bass riff that introduces this song. Other than that, it is presented as per the original from *Vagabonds*.

'Whisky In The Jar' (5:30): Another song that was previously only available as a cut-down radio-friendly single, but here we have the full-length version. Only now does it become apparent what a hatchet job they did on the single; at 2:48 it jumps from the middle of the solo, missing out a minute and a half to go straight to the last verse, without paying much attention to timing or finesse. Teamed with an earlier and quicker fadeout, this means the single saved about two minutes in all, sadly missing out the reference to a 'dirty old town' we get to hear on this version. The allusion is to a 1949 song about Salford in the North of England named 'Dirty Old Town', written by Ewan MacColl, which Lynott later covered during the sessions for *The Philip Lynott Album*, although it didn't make the cut. It has been covered by several

Irish musicians over the years and is now much more associated with Dublin than with Salford.

'The Rocker' (5:12): Originally from *Vagabonds,* except that in this version, Bell's entire two and a half minute solo is edited out. It's still a bit of an epic at five minutes, but the original was better.

The Continuing Saga Of The Ageing Orphans

Decca's belated follow-up to the highly successful *Remembering Part 1* was released in September 1979, less than six months after *Black Rose.* This time, they didn't just trot out a selection of the old Decca numbers; the songs are remixed and members of Thin Lizzy actively participated in giving some of the old songs a new lease of life by overdubbing guitar parts and redoing backing vocals. The result is another essential collection for Thin Lizzy completists, as these reworkings are not found on any other vinyl. Needless to say, they too would resurface on the expanded CD editions of the old albums, but the vinyl has been out of print for some time. This makes it indispensable that we examine the eleven tracks to some extent at least, as below. As for the cover art, Jim Fitzpatrick is active again, with a full-face portrait of Lynott taking up most of the frame; the five Decca albums including this one and *Remembering Part 1* are shown flying in like magic carpets from the top-left, most recent first – which means we actually see the *Ageing Orphans* cover as part of the *Ageing Orphans* cover. Pretty neat. Incidentally, Lizzy's song 'Saga Of The Ageing Orphan' doesn't actually appear in this collection. Again, we will have a look at the tracklisting, as it includes some genuinely new material.

'Things Ain't Working Out Down On The Farm' (3:58): Originally from the *New Day* EP, later on, expanded vinyl and CD editions of the self-titled debut album. In this version, the harmony vocals are re-done and Eric Bell's guitars are replaced with a much harder-rocking interpretation by Midge Ure. It's a shame really, Bell's imaginative fills and wah pedal work are lost here, but there's no doubt that the rockier version sounds less dated, with some nice answer-back soloing at the end.

'Buffalo Gal' (5:11): Originally from *Shades Of A Blue Orphanage,* this one is not heavily reworked, although a 20-second slice is removed from the middle, going straight from one verse to the next without repeating the bridge.

'Sarah' (2:48): Also originally from *Orphanage,* the bird song, which was probably too quiet anyway, has been removed from the intro, so it starts on Clodagh Simonds' ethereal piano, with a splash of cymbal added. Gary Moore adds some sweet lead guitar over the top, including some tastefully-controlled feedback over the intro and a beautiful, bluesy solo.

'Honesty Is No Excuse' (2:45): Originally from the first album. The only change in this track is that they fade it out a minute early. As it's an almost purely vocal track, it just dives out while Lynott is pontificating, which seems a bit rude.

'Look What the Wind Blew In' (3:22): OK, it's a bit of a weird one this one. The original arrangement has not been changed at all, and every single note of Bell's soloing and nifty little fills remains intact, but the guitar sound is better, and not just by a hair's breadth, it's miles better. There are places in the rhythm where it appears that another guitar has been thrown into the mix, but I would have to conclude that it's mostly Bell's original guitar work, heavily tweaked.

'Mama Nature Said' (4:52): As per the original on *Vagabonds*.

'The Hero And The Madman' (6:08): Again, as per the original on *Vagabonds*.

'Slow Blues' (4:46): Originally from *Vagabonds*, Eric Bell's imaginative funky rhythm work and restrained, BB King-inspired soloing is replaced by Gary Moore's more bluesy backing and up-front solo work – with its long feedback sustained notes, it draws heavily on Peter Green's instrumental 'Supernatural' from his days with the Bluesbreakers. Bell's single-guitar outro and the big crash ending are removed, taking half a minute off the end of the track.

'Dublin' (2:32): From the *New Day* EP, and later on both vinyl and CD expanded versions of *Thin Lizzy*. Quite a serious reworking of this one; the basic guitar fingerstyle track and vocals are left intact, but Clodagh Simonds' evocative celeste work is replaced with big, Wishbone Ash styled guitars, three in harmony. It's a great rendition, but very different from the original.

'Brought Down' (3:08): Again, Bell's proggy guitar work from *Orphanage* is replaced with more fashionable harder-rocking and powerful chordage, and over a minute's worth of soloing is simply edited out, making the track noticeably shorter.

'Vagabond Of The Western World' (4:46): The title track from *Vagabonds* of course, this too is left as per the original.

The Adventures Of... Thin Lizzy
This was the first official greatest hits collection since the move to Vertigo – the band even did a tour to promote it, propelling the album to a creditable no. 6 in the UK charts. Sub-titled 'The Hit-Singles Collection' and released in the UK and Ireland only in March 1981, it included eleven songs encompassing the

period from 'Whisky In The Jar' (which was a Decca release) down to 'Killer On The Loose' on *Chinatown*. Jim Fitzpatrick's screamingly bright cover art plays up Lynott's western obsession at last to the full, the words 'Thin Lizzy' riddled with bullet holes as the desperate banditos ride into a flaring sunset. The same tracklist was released in Germany only as *V.I.P. (Very Important Productions)* with a Snowy White era band photo on the front, and also widely released in Europe (including Germany), the Antipodes and elsewhere as *Lizzy Killers* with just the band name and album title on the cover. America, sadly, had pretty much forgotten about Thin Lizzy by this time.

Thin Lizzy – The Boys Are Back In Town
A low-priced compilation on the budget Pickwick label, this album was released in November 1983 and contained Vertigo material plus some obscure B-sides such as 'Half Caste' ('Rosalie'), 'Me And The Boys' ('Rosalie' live), 'Don't Play Around ('Killer On The Loose'), and 'Memory Pain' ('Trouble Boys').

The Collection
Released in November 1985, this 20-track gatefold double-LP of Decca material was the last official Thin Lizzy album prior to Lynott's death in January 1986. Within six months, they would find themselves having to release another one.

Whisky In The Jar
Barring a double Decca album named *Remembering* released only in Germany, this cheapo Pickwick UK-only twelve-track compilation of Decca material in April 1986 was the first official Thin Lizzy album after Lynott's death in January.

Soldier Of Fortune – The Best of Phil Lynott and Thin Lizzy
Surprisingly, it took until November 1987 before anyone released a compilation of the late Lynott's output, and this one was on Telstar, another budget label, the first of the compilations cross-pollinating Lizzy's output with other material featuring Lynott. Composed of material all the way from the Eric Bell era right down to Snowy White, it contained a number of songs that were not strictly Thin Lizzy at all: 'Parisienne Walkways', although featuring Lynott and Downey, was taken from Gary Moore's 1979 album *Back On The Streets,* and 'Out In The Fields' was taken from Moore's 1985 album *Run For Cover,* although it was officially released as a single by Gary Moore and Phil Lynott. It also contained the Decca single 'Whisky In The Jar', Lynott's solo tracks 'Yellow Pearl' and 'King's Call' and some live Thin Lizzy material. The album went gold in the UK, reaching no. 55 in the album chart, but was only released in the UK – not even Ireland.

Dedication: The Very Best of Thin Lizzy
Incredibly, it took until February 1991 before the powers-that-be eventually coughed up a decent celebration of Lynott's life and work in the UK and Europe, and a couple of months longer until, at last, a US release. Shockingly,

this Vertigo compilation, which reached no. 8 in the UK, still saw no release in Ireland. Billed as a Thin Lizzy compilation, it did not contain any of Lynott's solo material, but still retained the two famous Gary Moore songs on which Lynott sang. The compilation also included, of course, the song 'Dedication', which was originally an unreleased demo by Grand Slam. Archer's guitar was reportedly replaced and drums were added by Downey, enabling the piece to be included on this compilation as a Thin Lizzy song – see the 'Associated material' section for the *Thunder And Lightning* album.

Phil Lynott: The Man And His Music

OK, so this 1994 offering is a bootleg compilation – nevertheless, it collects more rare, unreleased, demo Phil Lynott songs than any other collection yet, from Skid Row all the way through to Lynott's solo material. It's on seven CDs, the majority of it is from the Thin Lizzy years and we won't even attempt to list all the songs – the word is that there is a ton of unreleased material out there, and it will doubtless keep coming out of the woodwork for years to come.

Wild One: The Very Best Of Thin Lizzy

Released in January 1996 as a ten-year commemoration of Lynott's death, this album was available in single or two-CD versions. The main disc, of course, included 'Parisienne Walkways' and 'Out In The Fields', even though these were not strictly Thin Lizzy recordings, and 'Whisky In The Jar' from the Decca days. The bonus disc comprised all six live songs from the full-length Canadian version of the *Killers Live* EP, plus the four live songs from the *Thunder And Lightning* limited edition bonus EP.

The Boys Are Back In Town

Released in December 2000 in Sweden only, with a limited release of 20,000 copies, this two-CD set is notable mostly for disc two. OK, disc one is great, adding Lynott's 'Solo In Soho' and 'King's Call' to a stellar list of classic Lizzy songs, but the eight-track disc two includes some real obscurities: non-album singles, obscure B-sides and even the Greedies' Christmas single 'A Merry Jingle'. The compilation itself was a labour of love by Swedish fans, but even better, it used an absolutely stonking cover painting by Jim Fitzpatrick of the band in action, all flaring spotlights, dry ice and rocking action. The painting was originally created for a mooted album named Lizzy *Killers* in about 1981 which never materialised, and was effectively lost to the public until the Swedes unearthed it and used it for this rare compilation. (In fact *The Adventures Of... Thin Lizzy* compilation was released in several countries under the name *Lizzy Killers* but did not use this cover art. Neither did the *Live Killers* EP.) Universal Music in Denmark used the same album title and cover art for a completely different compilation in 2010, a more conventional but massive 36-track double-disc set.

Vagabonds Kings Warriors Angels

Released in December 2001, this one is all you need really, for official releases at least; a massive 4-CD retrospective covering pretty much everything, with a detailed, lusciously-illustrated booklet. Disc one (subtitled 'Vagabonds') contains eighteen songs from the first single 'The Farmer' through to songs from *Vagabonds*. Disc two (subtitled 'Kings') pulls out some singles from the first Gary Moore era, then the Vertigo days through to the *Jailbreak* album. Disc three (subtitled 'Warriors') is mostly *Johnny The Fox* and *Black Rose* plus a few bonuses. Disc four (subtitled 'Angels') covers the Snowy White and John Sykes eras, plus Lynott's solo work, right down to his last single 'Nineteen'. The selection includes the first-ever CD outings for such songs as 'Cruising In The Lizzymobile', 'Try A Little Harder' and 'Song For Jimi'.

The Greatest Hits

A double-CD 36-track collection released in June 2004 by Universal, which climbed to an astounding number three on the UK charts and went triple-platinum in Ireland. It only includes 'Whisky In The Jar' and 'The Rocker' from the Decca days, but also adds a fair smattering of Lynott solo material, plus the usual Gary Moore pair, with previously-unreleased live versions of 'Cowboy Song' and 'The Boys Are Back In Town' from the Sydney Harbour gig.

Rock Legends

After these releases, there was a veritable avalanche of collections, mostly re-treads of the Decca material, in various countries. The last notable compilation at the time of writing is this sumptuous 50th anniversary box set, which was announced on 20 August 2020, on what would have been Phil Lynott's 71st birthday. Comprising six CDs, one DVD, a hardback book and sundry other memorabilia, it crams no fewer than 74 previously unreleased recordings into a total of 99 tracks. While most are rare edits of known songs, live versions, radio sessions, demos and the like, it also includes some genuinely unknown new songs from across the band's history. At the time of publication, this collection had not been released.

Other notable recordings

Gradually, of course, more and more material is seeping out. *The Peel Sessions* was released in 1994, containing live-in-the-studio recordings made for several episodes of John Peel's show on BBC Radio 1, throughout the history of the band. All of these and more were also included on the eight-disc *Thin Lizzy At The BBC* collection in 2011, containing both CD and DVD material. More and more live recordings have been released, some of which have already been mentioned, but perhaps most notably *Still Dangerous* in March 2009 on the VH1 Classic label. This comprised recordings from the October 1977 gigs at the Tower Theatre in Philadelphia, USA, which contributed some of the material for *Live And Dangerous*. Lynott was a prolific songwriter though, and made an undetermined number of home and studio recordings with any number of collaborators, both Thin Lizzy-related and otherwise. Huge caches of such material are reported to exist, so it can be expected that previously-unreleased songs will gradually see the light of day for decades to come.

Bibliography
Books
Haze, X. *Emerald Rebels: The Rise, Fall and Redemption of Philip Lynott and Thin Lizzy* (USA: Alima Press, 2015)

Thomson, G. *Cowboy Song – The Authorised Biography Of Phil Lynott* (UK: Constable, 2016)

Putterford, M. *Philip Lynott: The Rocker* (UK: Omnibus Press, 2002)

Planet Rock magazine (Issue 7, May 2018)

Rock Society magazine (issue 230, May/June 2019)

Internet Resources

www.allmusic.com

www.barrymccabe.com

www.discogs.com

www.genius.com

www.guitarplayer.com (Matt Blackett 6 Feb 2012)

www.heavymetalrarities.com

www.irelandsown.ie

www.irishcentral.com

www.irishmirror.ie

www.irishrock.org

www.jimfitzpatrick.com

www.last.fm

www.loudersound.com

www.metal-archives.com

www.officialcharts.com

www.reverb.com

www.songmeanings.com

www.songfacts.com

www.thoughtco.com

www.trcjt.ca

www.thinlizzy.org

www.wikipedia.org

A special round of applause for Peter Nielsen's excellent www.thinlizzyguide. com

Dream Theater - *on track*

every album, every song

Dream Theater - on track
every album, every song
Jordan Blum
Paperback
160 pages
41 colour photographs
978-1-78952-050-7
£14.99
USD 21.95

Every album produced by the world's best-known progressive metal band.

No other band has affected modern progressive metal as deeply or widely as American quintet Dream Theater. Formed at Berklee College of Music as Majesty in 1985 by guitarist John Petrucci, drummer Mike Portnoy, and bassist John Myung, the group has spent thirty years repeatedly pushing new boundaries and reinventing their identity. Although other acts – such as Queensrÿche and Fates Warning – paved the way for the prog-metal subgenre, Dream Theater were without doubt the first to meld influences from both metal and progressive rock into a groundbreaking blend of quirky instrumentation, extensively complex arrangements, and exceptional songwriting. Whether subtly or overtly, they've since left their mark on just about every progressive metal band that's followed.

In this book, Jordan Blum examines virtually all Dream Theater collections, and their behind-the-scenes circumstances, to explore how the group distinctively impacted the genre with each release. Whether classics of the 1990s like *Images and Words* and *Metropolis Pt. 2: Scenes from a Memory*, benchmarks of the 2000s like *Six Degrees of Inner Turbulence* and *Octavarium*, or even thrilling modern efforts like *A Dramatic Turn of Events* and *Distance Over Time*, every sequence of albums contributes something crucial to making Dream Theater's legacy nothing short of astonishing.

The Who - *on track*

every album, every song

The Who - on track
every album, every song
Geoffrey Feakes
Paperback
176 pp
42 colour photographs
978-1-78952-076-7
£14.99
USD 21.95

Every album produced by one of the world's best-selling - and most controversial - rock bands.

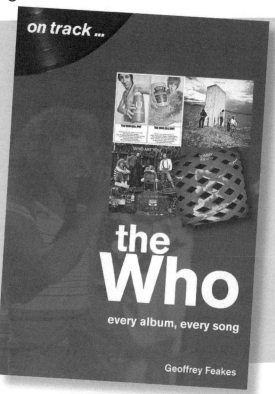

Formed in 1964 and still going strong in 2020, the Who are one of the most popular and enduring bands in the history of rock. The legendary debut album *My Generation* and a string of hit singles paved the way for Live At Leeds, hailed as the best live rock album of all time, and the best selling *Who's Next*. Powered by the phenomenal rhythm section of Keith Moon and John Entwistle, they earned a reputation as a premier live act and pioneered festival and arena performances. The rock operas *Tommy* and *Quadrophenia* took popular music into uncharted territories and both inspired hit films. Despite regular infighting, breakups and the death of two key members, the band continued into the 21st century with the well received *Endless Wire* album and original members Roger Daltrey and Pete Townshend stage spectacular live shows to this day.

This book examines each one of the band's studio albums, including the latest Who released in December 2019. Non-album tracks are also included and the book traces the band's long and diverse history. Compilations, live albums and soundtracks are also discussed, making this the most comprehensive guide to the music of the Who yet published. Whether the reader is a diehard fan or someone curious to see what lies beyond *Tommy*, this is essential reading.

10cc - *on track*

every album, every song

10cc and Godley and Creme -
on track
every album, every song
Peter Kearns
Paperback
176 pages
42 colour photographs
978-1-78952-054-5
US ISBN: 978-1-78952-075-0
£14.99
USD 21.95

Every album produced by this cult British band - and offshoot duo Kevin Godley and Lol Creme.

Hailing from Manchester, England, sophisticated pop purveyors 10cc hit the ground running with their 1972 debut single, 'Donna'. Their pedigree reached back to bassist Graham Gouldman's '60s' songwriting successes including The Yardbirds' 'For Your Love' and The Hollies' 'Bus Stop'. Guitarist and recording engineer, Eric Stewart, was already a bonafide pop star having sung the global 1966 hit, 'Groovy Kind of Love', for his group The Mindbenders. When the pair teamed up with drummer/singer Kevin Godley and multi-instrumentalist/singer, Lol Creme, the combination wrought a legacy of four albums. They included the ambitious *The Original Soundtrack* and several hit singles, including the

groundbreaking 'I'm Not In Love,' that were rich in eclectic boundary-pushing pop that earned 10cc comparisons to The Beatles while still occupying a unique position in music.

Departing in 1976, Godley and Creme moved on to create genre-defying experimental albums, while Gouldman and Stewart continued their run of hit singles and albums with a new 10cc lineup. Their final album was 1995's, *Mirror Mirror*, a highly respectable full stop on the influential band's colourful and innovative discography. This book examines every released recording by both Godley & Creme and 10cc, including the band's debut album under their early name, Hotlegs.

Mike Oldfield - *on track*

every album, every song

Mike Oldfield - on track
every album, every song
Ryan Yard
Paperback
176 pages
42 colour photographs
978-1-78952-060-6
£14.99
USD 21.95

Every album produced by one of the most enigmatic and talented solo artists of the 1970s.

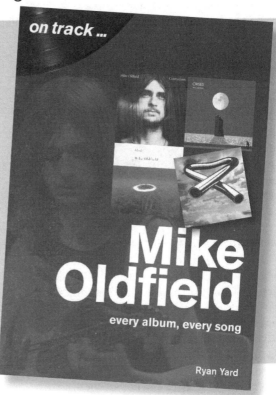

It can be difficult for an artist to have such overwhelming success so early into their career as was the case for Mike Oldfield. To this day, his name is forever synonymous with the album *Tubular Bells*. Mike followed this album with three further long form works in the 1970s, before venturing off onto other musical paths. The 1980s saw further success both in the albums and singles charts, while recent years have seen a return to long form music, often via sequels to his most famous work, with his most recent album being *Return To Ommadawn* in 2017.

The music of Mike Oldfield touches listeners in ways that can be hard to describe. It bridges the gap between many musical cultures, whilst staying sharp and alert to current technological trends. In this book, Ryan Yard looks at the entire catalogue of albums to uncover what it is that makes his music so special. Each track from every album is critiqued with the aim of offering long term fans a different perspective whilst enticing new fans to explore and familiarise themselves with such wonderful new music. It makes a wonderful companion as the listener absorbs the music, hopefully offering food for thought as they embark on, or continue, their journey through the music of this remarkable artist.

On Track series

Queen – Andrew Wild 978-1-78952-003-3
Emerson Lake and Palmer – Mike Goode 978-1-78952-000-2
Deep Purple and Rainbow 1968-79 – Steve Pilkington 978-1-78952-002-6
Yes – Stephen Lambe 978-1-78952-001-9
Blue Oyster Cult – Jacob Holm-Lupo 978-1-78952-007-1
The Beatles – Andrew Wild 978-1-78952-009-5
Roy Wood and the Move – James R Turner 978-1-78952-008-8
Genesis – Stuart MacFarlane 978-1-78952-005-7
Jethro Tull – Jordan Blum 978-1-78952-016-3
The Rolling Stones 1963-80 – Steve Pilkington 978-1-78952-017-0
Judas Priest – John Tucker 978-1-78952-018-7
Toto – Jacob Holm-Lupo 978-1-78952-019-4
Van Der Graaf Generator – Dan Coffey 978-1-78952-031-6
Frank Zappa 1966 to 1979 – Eric Benac 978-1-78952-033-0
Elton John in the 1970s – Peter Kearns 978-1-78952-034-7
The Moody Blues – Geoffrey Feakes 978-1-78952-042-2
The Beatles Solo 1969-1980 – Andrew Wild 978-1-78952-030-9
Steely Dan – Jez Rowden 978-1-78952-043-9
Hawkwind – Duncan Harris 978-1-78952-052-1
Fairport Convention – Kevan Furbank 978-1-78952-051-4
Iron Maiden – Steve Pilkington 978-1-78952-061-3
Dream Theater – Jordan Blum 978-1-78952-050-7
10CC and Godley and Crème – Peter Kearns 978-1-78952-054-5
Gentle Giant – Gary Steel 978-1-78952-058-3
Kansas – Kevin Cummings 978-1-78952-057-6
Mike Oldfield – Ryan Yard 978-1-78952-060-6
The Who – Geoffrey Feakes 978-1-78952-076-7
Crosby, Stills and Nash – Andrew Wild 978-1-78952-039-2
U2 – Eoghan Lyng 978-1-78952-078-1
Barclay James Harvest – Keith and Monika Domone 978-1-78952-067-5
Steve Hackett – Geoffrey Feakes 978-1-78952-098-9
Renaissance – David Detmer 978-1-78952-062-0
Dire Straits – Andrew Wild 978-1-78952-044-6
Camel – Hamish Kuzminski 978-1-78952-040-8
Rush – Will Romano 978-1-78952-080-4
Joni Mitchell – Peter Kearns 978-1-78952-081-1
UFO – Richard James 978-1-78952-073-6
Kate Bush – Bill Thomas 978-1-78952-097-2
Asia – Pete Braidis 978-1-78952-099-6
Aimee Mann – Jez Rowden 978-1-78952-036-1
Pink Floyd Solo – Mike Goode 978-1-78952-046-0
Gong – Kevan Furbank 978-1-78952-082-8

Decades Series
Pink Floyd in the 1970s – Georg Purvis 978-1-78952-072-9
Marillion in the 1980s – Nathaniel Webb 978-1-78952-065-1
Focus in the 1970s – Stephen Lambe 978-1-78952-079-8
Curved Air in the 1970s – Laura Shenton 978-1-78952-069-9

On Screen series
Carry On... – Stephen Lambe 978-1-78952-004-0
Seinfeld Seasons 1 to 5 – Stephen Lambe 978-1-78952-012-5
Monty Python – Steve Pilkington 978-1-78952-047-7
Doctor Who: The David Tennant Years – Jamie Hailstone 978-1-78952-066-8
James Bond – Andrew Wild 978-1-78952-010-1
David Cronenberg – Patrick Chapman 978-1-78952- 071-2

Other Books
Maximum Darkness – Deke Leonard 978-1-78952-048-4
The Twang Dynasty – Deke Leonard 978-1-78952-049-1
Tommy Bolin: In and Out of Deep Purple – Laura Shenton 978-1-78952-070-5
Jon Anderson and the Warriors - the road to Yes – David Watkinson 978-1-78952-059-0
Derek Taylor: For Your Radioactive Children - Andrew Darlington 978-1-78952-038-5
20 Walks Around Tewkesbury – Stephen Lambe 978-1-78952-074-3

and many more to come!

Would you like to write for Sonicbond Publishing?

We are mainly a music publisher, but we also occasionally publish in other genres including film and television. At Sonicbond Publishing we are always on the look-out for authors, particularly for our two main series.

On Track. Mixing fact with in depth analysis, the On Track series examines the entire recorded work of a particular musical artist or group. All genres are considered from easy listening and jazz to 60s soul to 90s pop, via rock and metal.

Decades. This series singles out a particular decade in an artist or group's history and focuses on that decade in more detail than may be allowed in the On Track series.

While professional writing experience would, of course, be an advantage, the most important qualification is to have real enthusiasm and knowledge of your subject. First-time authors are welcomed, but the ability to write well in English is essential.

Sonicbond Publishing has distribution throughout Europe and North America, and all our books are also published in E-book form. Authors will be paid a royalty based on sales of their book. Further details about our books are available from www.sonicbondpublishing.com. To contact us, complete the contact form there or email info@sonicbondpublishing.co.uk